EDINBURGH
UNDER
SIEGE
1571-1573

EDINBURGH
UNDER
SIEGE
1571-1573

HARRY POTTER

TEMPUS

First published 2003

Tempus Publishing Ltd
The Mill, Brimscombe Port
Stroud, Gloucestershire GL5 2QG
www.tempus-publishing.com

British Library Cataloguing in Publication Data.
A catalogue record for this book is available from the British Library.

ISBN 0 7524 2332 0

Typesetting and origination by Tempus Publishing
Printed in Great Britain

CONTENTS

PREFACE

No sooner had I finished one book on Scottish history, *Blood Feud*, than my publishers were pestering me for another. They were doing a series on Scottish battles and suggested Culloden, but I thought that that battle had, as it were, been done to death. I wanted something a little less clichéd – I found it in the fate of Edinburgh in the early 1570s. The English Civil War is well known, much researched, and often the subject of film and television documentary. The Marian or – as it may be called – Scottish Civil War, which lasted almost as long, is practically forgotten even amongst as nostalgic a group as we Scots. Many books do not refer to these turbulent events as a civil war, and while the fall of Edinburgh Castle in 1573 marks the end of the matter, there is no obvious starting point. Some would date its beginning with the assassination of Moray in 1570, others with the deposition of the Queen in 1567. I favour the latter position, but accept that the divisions become much clearer and deeply rooted in the latter period. Whatever its parameters, a civil war there was, between the supporters of the deposed Mary Queen of Scots (the 'Marians') and the adherents of the infant King James (the 'Jacobeans') – and one that ravaged the country and enveloped its major city over the course of several years. This book concerns that conflict, and in particular the fate of Edinburgh, town and Castle, during the 'Long Siege' of 1571-1573.

There is wealth of ready documentation on the subject and, as usual, my thanks must go to the great libraries that facilitated my researches: the British Library, the Cambridge University Library, the St Andrews University Library and Edinburgh City Library. Many individuals and institutions kindly consented to the use of their material as illustrations. They receive due credit here. As a Scot I am pleased to say that our reputation for parsimony is misplaced. Not only have the staff of Scottish institutions such as the Scottish National Galleries, Museums and Libraries been outstandingly helpful, they have often waived any fees or reduced them. So too did the City of Edinburgh Libraries. Individuals such as Lord Egremont and the Duke

1   Maitland of Lethington, the grand old man of Scottish politics.

of Abercorn were equally generous. Alas, the spirit of Thatcherite business acumen seems much more alive in institutions south of the Border. Even photocopying and photography are significantly cheaper the further north you go.

My publishers have been consistently enthusiastic, and my patient and long-suffering friends, Andy and Dorothy Butters, make good proof-readers and excellent critics. Faults in the text, and failings in its construction are, of course, mine.

2 The only extant – but doubtful – portrait of Kirkcaldy of Grange. The subject has a rather debonair, almost French appearance.

INTRODUCTION

'[Edinburgh Castle] was called the Maiden Castle because it resisted every
attack, and women never do.'[1]

As William Kirkcaldy of Grange, Captain of Edinburgh Castle, swung on the
rope that was strangling him, his purpling face turning inexorably westwards
towards the setting sun, it is not hard to believe that his thoughts also turned, as
the divines suggested, to the prophetic death-bed denunciation of that dour
Ezekiel of Scotland, John Knox. As his old friend had predicted, Grange had been
torn like an eagle from his rocky lair and immolated in the face of the sun, like
some sacrifice irradiated to a savage deity. William Maitland of Lethington,
Grange's co-consul in the duumvirate of the Marian party in Scotland, to the last
living up to his contemporary sobriquet as the Scots Machiavelli, had escaped the
noose or the block by dying in the Tolbooth at Leith. It was reported he had
'hast[ed] the same himself' by swallowing poison 'after the old Roman fashion,'
but this may have been a slander of enemies deprived of their greatest prey. He
had been ill for years and dying by inches. Whatever occasioned Lethington's
demise, it is unlikely that his last thoughts were of John Knox or any other divine.

So ended the lives of the two great champions of Mary Queen of Scots who
had lost her throne by folly, her liberty by impetuosity, and who would lose her
head by duplicity. Her son James had replaced her, and his partisans had
triumphed. Mary's cause, however, was not hopeless when Grange and
Lethington first championed it, but their double demise sealed its fate
irredeemably. The two Williams were unlikely friends and equally unlikely
champions of a Catholic Queen whose defeat and disgrace they had originally
helped instigate and engineer.

William Kirkcaldy of Grange was the eldest son of James Kirkcaldy, a
Fifeshire laird, who had been High Treasurer of Scotland under James V. From

his early years William was a staunch Protestant who had been one of the leading players in the murder of Cardinal Beaton at St Andrews Castle in 1547. There he had undergone a two-month siege, a siege brought to an end, not by the ineffectual barrage of the Scottish cannon, but by the arrival of French ordnance, gunners and troops. On its surrender he had been sent to the galleys and served at the oars with John Knox himself. Grange was by temperament a man of violent action and a fine professional soldier. He became a particular favourite of the King of France in whose armies he served with distinction. Mercenary he may have been, but he was a patriotic and Protestant Scot first. In 1559 when the French came to Leith to aid the Catholic cause, he greatly distinguished himself against them and is said to have slain the first foreign intruder in a hand-to-hand encounter. During the first few years of Mary's reign Grange took no part in public affairs, but after the disquiet of the Darnley marriage he served loyally the Lords of the Congregation, the military wing of the Protestant party in Scotland. He fought against Mary at Carberry. He acquiesced in the Queen relinquishing the throne to her baby son, James VI, and insisted she relinquish her rapacious consort, Bothwell. For his loyalty and ability, Grange was appointed by the Regent Moray to the crucial post of Keeper of Edinburgh Castle. He was, in short, a principal deviser, and one of the most vital bastions, of the new regime.

By contrast to this man of military prowess, William Maitland of Lethington was an enormously gifted civil servant and wily politician, a man of words, winning battles by intellect, subterfuge and cunning. Queen Elizabeth described him as the 'the flower of the wits of Scotland', and, when she heard that Sussex had outwitted him in a literary encounter, said she was more pleased than she would be had he won a battle in the field. Bannatyne – no fan – dubbed William 'the great god, the secretary.'[2] It was one of those insults that the object of it relishes. Lethington's origins were somewhat less than divine. He was the eldest son of Sir Richard Maitland of Lethington, a lawyer and a poet and a patriot, a scion of an old family of no particular distinction, long settled in the area between Edinburgh and the Border. William was a rarity in his day for being a true sceptic, even a cynic in matters of religion. At the very least he was dangerously moderate. As a politician he thought exclusively in secular and rationalist terms and was dismissive of the views and influence of the preachers.[3] He had a sharp tongue and was prepared to use it against the Reformers. Knox denounced him as a mocker and an atheist who had said that heaven and hell are 'things devised to make bairns afraid.' He was capable of taking on Knox at theological debate and treating him as an equal.[4] Though he could and would speak with contemptuous disregard of such

Protestant fanatics, he had no greater attachment to the old faith. The dominant motif in his political philosophy – as of his life – was the union of England and Scotland as equals. He began his career as Secretary to Mary of Guise and served her well so long as she followed a policy of conciliation and toleration. As soon as her policy changed to one of subjugation to France he broke with her and became the chief diplomat for the Lords of the Congregation in their fight for independence from the French. In this role he was vital in securing the support of Elizabeth for the Protestants. With the return of Mary Stuart to claim her throne, Lethington again flourished since both concurred in the ultimate aim: union of the two crowns. He remained Secretary, the most senior government minister, throughout her reign. Just five months before Carberry the ties between them became closer with his marriage to one of her ladies in waiting, Mary Fleming, in January 1567. Although his services to his Queen extended to plotting the murder of her husband Darnley – at her behest or even with her connivance – he deserted her when she married her husband's murderer, Bothwell. This impulsive act of an infatuated woman dashed her hopes of ever uniting the crowns. He joined the coalition against her, but in his, as in Grange's case, it was to rid his Queen of her troublesome spouse, not to rid the nation of its Queen. He had no desire to ruin her or force her to abdicate. But so long as she remained devoted to Bothwell he could see no other way than to supplant her – temporarily – with her son.

It was this unlikely pair – a soldier and a civil servant – who, when others failed, held out to the bitter end in her forlorn cause, fighting a vicious civil war, and hoping always for that elusive triumph which would vanquish their opponents and deliver their Queen. They had two characteristics in common: courage and obduracy, the former necessary for their struggle, the latter fatal to it.

The centre of Marian resistance was the town of Edinburgh and its Castle. The capital city was the seat of central government, the Castle the first fortress and principal armoury of the kingdom. Together they were the heart and nerve-centre of Scotland. In addition Dumbarton in the west was a Marian stronghold and great swathes of the country were under the complete control of Marian magnates: Argyll and his Campbells had their vast empire in the west; Huntly and his Gordons ruled unchallenged in the north-east; the Hamiltons dominated Glasgow and the south-western lowlands; and brigand barons, such as Walter Scott of Buccleugh and Lord Home, roamed unchecked in the Borders. The Queen's cause prospered and the King's men made their beleaguered resistance, centred not in Edinburgh but, humiliatingly, in its port

3 This panoramic view of Edinburgh was first published in 1582, but may have been based on information from an earlier drawing of 1573. The only building named is the Castrum Puellarum, or Maiden Castle. The city gates and the Nor Loch are clearly shown. Craigmillar Castle may be the building on the hill to the south-east.

of Leith. There, Regent after Regent plotted and planned, and pleaded with England for help. From there they launched ever more desperate raids on Edinburgh, all repulsed and their efforts derided. Yet it was the King's party that finally vanquished. Why and how are the questions behind this book.

In the following pages I shall trace the changing contours of the Marian Civil War, focusing primarily on Edinburgh and its environs, but with a weather eye to the rest of the country. I shall try to describe what took place and what might have been from a contemporary point of view, uncoloured by our knowledge of the final denouement. An impossible task, I suspect, but a means of maintaining the high drama of a civil war whose course is little known, whose end was never certain, and whose consequences were so drastic for the history of our nation.

I

HURTLING TOWARDS DISASTER
August 1561 to August 1567

This traitor tyrant of our time,
This Satan's seed, I mean
This rebel Regent...
This perfect pattern of deceit.

Tom Truth
'A Rhyme in Defence of the Queen of Scots against the Earl of Moray.'[1]

The unhappy reign of Mary Queen of Scots lasted only six years and went from bad to worse. She began oddly, embarking on a progress to the north which led in 1562 to the rebellion, defeat and death of George Gordon, fourth Earl of Huntly, the leading Catholic peer in the realm.[2] His fall was accompanied by the rise of his great rival, the Queen's illegitimate half brother, James Stewart, the Earl of Moray.

The marriage of Mary to Lord Darnley, three years later, while entirely understandable in dynastic terms, uniting as it did two near claims to the throne of England, was inspired as much by lust as by policy, and soon proved disastrous. Within months the Queen loathed him and, after his participation in the murder of her secretary David Ricchio, despised and feared him. But he was the father still of the baby born in June 1566, James, the heir to her throne and England's. The Queen was in a quandary. To annul the marriage would make that heir a bastard, and, as a Catholic, she could not countenance divorce. She retreated into a state of nervous breakdown, hysterically talked of suicide, and threw herself into the hands of her courtiers. At Craigmillar in November 1566 the council under her Secretary Lethington promised to rid the Queen of the problem. The fate of Darnley was sealed. On 10 February

1567 he was murdered at his house in Kirk o' Field. Three months later Mary married again, her choice being James Hepburn, the fourth Earl of Bothwell, and the prime suspect in her previous husband's murder.

The country was outraged, and virtually all the nobility were alienated. To replace a feckless and ineffectual youth with a brutal ruffian and regicide as the active ruler of their Queen and so of the country was too much to bear. Some privately relished an opportunity to be rid of this Papist whore of a Queen. Others such as Lethington and Kirkcaldy of Grange believed in the official line and wanted to rescue her from herself and her spouse. Grange, the kingdom's greatest general, concluded that 'the Queen will never cease till she has wrecked all the honest men of this realm.' He believed – or at least repeated – the reports that she had wished Bothwell to ravish her, so that she would have the pretext of marrying him to preserve her honour. Mary was intending to put Prince James into the hands of the man who had murdered his father. This threat to the royal line could not be countenanced. The Queen had to be saved from herself. Grange joined the Lords of the Congregation, while Lethington betrayed to them all her plans. Moray kept his hands clean and his options open by staying out of the country.[3]

Seeking security, Mary and Bothwell tried to gain entry into Edinburgh Castle, but its gates were closed against them. They initially withdrew to Dunbar to weather the storm, but, before her supporters had time to rally, were prematurely tempted to leave this safe haven and seize the capital. The avenging forces of the Confederate Lords ranged against the Queen and her consort proved too great. Bearing banners depicting the slaughter of Darnley and crying for vengeance they blocked her way south of Edinburgh at Carberry Hill on Sunday 15 June 1567. Her inexperienced troops deserting in droves, she surrendered herself to Grange while Bothwell was allowed to make off. The Queen of Scots was brought captive through the streets of her capital, where the crowds subjected her to taunts and insults. In contravention of Grange's assurance, she was not brought to Holyrood, but to the Provost of Edinburgh's house where she was confined to a small room. The following day she was taken to the island prison of Lochleven. Grange accepted that so long as Bothwell was at large and she still attached to him, imprisoned she would have to be. Others would go further. She could be replaced. To them she was a liability and a danger as well as an embarrassment. Just as the birth of her son had made her first husband disposable, so the royal baby's healthy survival had rendered her dispensable. Abandoned by all, and in the midst of miscarrying twins, she was forced to abdicate on 24 July 1567, in favour of her baby son. Five days later James VI was crowned King. This was a deliberate and

4 A stunning portrait of the beautiful young Queen. It is not hard to imagine why she engendered such devotion.

determined act taken without consulting England and was the final nail in Mary's coffin. She had not merely abdicated, she had been supplanted. Edinburgh rejoiced over the coronation with near 1,000 bonfires and the Castle firing off a twenty gun salute. Perhaps the celebrations of its inhabitants would have been a little more subdued had they realised that for the next six years Scotland would be riven by civil war, between the followers of the young 'godly' prince and of his 'Papist' mother, and that, as citizens of the capital, they would be at the centre of the conflagration.

On 22 August 1567 the recently returned Earl of Moray, was proclaimed Regent – significantly with Mary's consent – and took up residence in Edinburgh Castle. Symbolising continuity and his quasi-regal authority, control of this citadel was vital to his regency. By a generous settlement the new Regent persuaded its Keeper, Sir James Balfour, a bosom friend of Bothwell, to deliver the first fortress of the land into his hands. For this kindness Balfour received assurances that he would face no prosecution for the murder of Darnley. Moray in turn intended to hand the Castle over into the safe keeping of his old friend and loyal ally, Kirkcaldy of Grange when he returned from the north.

Days before Moray's elevation, Grange had accepted a belated commission to pursue Bothwell. He had taken to this task with the alacrity of an avenging harpy since his reason for joining the Confederate Lords in the first place was to 'liberate' Mary and restore Scotland 'to liberty and honour, after this treasonable deed committed by that traitor Bothwell.'[4] Grange and another redoubtable soldier, Murray of Tullibardine, with three armed ships made after their prey, who had fled to his dukedom of Orkney and there, among the windswept islands, played pirate. Grange boasted he would either bring back the King's killer or die in the attempt. He did neither. His ship pursued the miscreant but struck upon a submerged rock and, in the frantic efforts to save men and ordnance, Bothwell's slighter vessel got away. But Bothwell was doomed. As impetuous as his wife, he fled to Norway, and a life of exile and imprisonment. Grange had wanted to rid the Queen of a baneful influence. This he had achieved. He returned south to find that far from being liberated from the trammels of an ill-judged marriage, she was being permanently supplanted by her own son and half brother.

It was completely unclear at the time what the implications of this were. It was a novel and unique circumstance. Things had gone much further than Grange or Lethington expected or would have wanted. Yet the door was not shut on the Queen's restoration, or even some form of joint rule with her son, when things had calmed down and she had got over Bothwell. Grange may well have wondered whether what he was witnessing was a constitutional upheaval or an ingenious stop-gap measure to ensure continuity in government and reassure the country. At any rate, a man he trusted, Moray, was in charge. The Regent understood the position of the likes of Grange and Lethington. The kingdom was in safe hands while a final resolution was worked out. Moray reciprocated the trust placed in him by immediately installing Grange in the key positions of Keeper of Edinburgh Castle and Provost of Edinburgh.

Edinburgh Castle was some prize for Grange. Popularly known as Maiden Castle it was the most impressive fortress in the land, covering six acres, dominating the town, and providing a secure centre for the government. Thomas Churchyard hymned it as 'This lofty seat and Lantern of that land/Like lode star stode, and lokte o'er ev'ry street.'[5] The heart of the Castle was the Upper Ward, set on the summit of the rock. David II erected a massive L-shaped three-storey tower, later named after him, soaring almost 100 feet above the eastern crags where the Half Moon Battery now stands, enclosing what remains. It was intended as a royal lodging as well as the principal defence towards the burgh. Its ground floor vault may have served as a strong-room of the Treasury where the crown jewels and national archives were kept. His successor, Robert II, further enhanced the tower by turning it into a massive rectangular keep. At the same time he built the main north-eastern gate tower on the site of the present Portcullis Gate. This fifty-foot high round tower was later called Constable's Tower because it became the residence of the Constable or Keeper. It was here that Grange would have had his quarters. A massive curtain wall (now the Forewell Battery), rebuilt in 1544 and loopholed for the heaviest artillery, connected the two great towers. Behind and above it lay yet another tier of ordnance. The entrance gate was further protected by a flanking bastion – later expanded into the Spur – and by a culverin and two smaller artillery pieces placed just inside the postern. In the fifteenth century the royal buildings were built in Palace Yard (now Crown Square), the principal courtyard constructed on great stone vaults on the south-facing slopes of Castle rock. The Palace stood on the east side, the Great Hall to the south, the Gunhouse – where the artillery was kept – on the west, and to the north, St Mary's Church which in 1540 became the Munition House (now the site of the National War Memorial). Another former ecclesiastical building – the ancient St Margaret's Chapel – was converted into a gunpowder magazine at the same time. The descent from the summit was by a long staircase or by a wide and winding road designed for the movement of heavy ordnance in and out of the Castle. The vaults themselves were used as stores, barracks, a

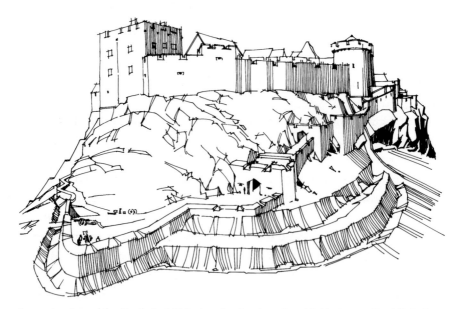

5 Reconstruction of the Castle in 1561, showing just how formidable it was. David's is the square tower on the left, Constable's the round one on the right. The Spur is prominent in the left foreground protecting the entrance.

bakehouse and as part of the arsenal. The Middle Ward was developed from the fifteenth century onwards as the workshop of the Castle where blacksmithing and other light industrial activities took place. There were two main sources of water, the Fore Well near David's Tower, which despite its depth could not sustain a garrison under siege, and St Margaret's Well at the foot of Castle Rock where it meets the Nor Loch. The latter was housed within the Wellhouse Tower which also served as the gatehouse to the western entry to the Outer Ward. Seventy feet above the tower was the Crane Seat, a stone platform from which to drop missiles on attackers.

In the years following the disastrous English incursions of the 1540s, every effort was made to render the Castle impregnable even from cannon fire. In particular an angular bulwark of *trace Italienne* design was constructed, later known as the Spur. This blockhouse was an advanced redoubt with enormously thick earthen ramparts twenty feet high, augmented by arrow-shaped bastions, projecting out over Castlehill where the Esplanade now lies. Stone served to face the ramparts and bastions and to support the gun platforms, but was otherwise supplanted by a packed earth and turf covering. Stone would shatter and crack when a cannon ball impacted, plain earth would swallow it up. The Spur had tunnel-like loops piercing greatly thickened walls of a scale generous enough to be armed with four cannons and two *gros culverins*.[6] It was so constructed that each face of the redoubt was covered by the guns on another part of the fortification. Following its construction, approach to the Castle was through the Spur. Behind it was the rampart between the two towers, and above that the second battery stretching between St Mary's and St Margaret's.

As the national armoury and ordnance factory, the Castle held the main munitions in the kingdom and the greatest cannon, including the huge bombard Mons Meg. In 1562 a 3-inch *culverin moyen* had been hoisted to the top of David's Tower and in 1565 four new $6\frac{1}{2}$-inch French cannon were mounted on the curtain wall on the east front. By 1566 the perimeter bristled with over twenty-five cast bronze guns. Two *gros culverins* were added to the four existing curtain cannon. Behind them, in the second eastward-facing tier between St Mary's Church and St Margaret's Chapel, were two *bastard culverins* and two other cannon. Two cannon and two 3-inch guns were on the north front, four pieces were near the western postern, and four more along the south front. In reserve there was a *gros culverin* and a *moyen* kept next to the great hall beside the Gunhouse gable. The age and quality was variable. Mons Meg was over 100 years old, and the inventory for 1567 included an English *gross culverin* 'auld and rottin', and several iron field pieces – two long serpentines and six lighter *cut-throats* – which had to be kept under cover.[7] Nonetheless this was the most formidable array of ordnance in all Scotland, augmented by Grange when he removed all the artillery, powder and bullets from Dunbar Castle and brought them safe into his own citadel. Perhaps they constituted the six cannon that were mounted on the recently completed Spur. The only guns in Scotland capable of reducing Edinburgh Castle were held firmly inside Edinburgh Castle. It was never envisaged that this could pose a problem.

6 The Castle in 1544 hugging the eastern part of the mount. David's and Constable's Towers can be clearly seen with the curtain wall between them.

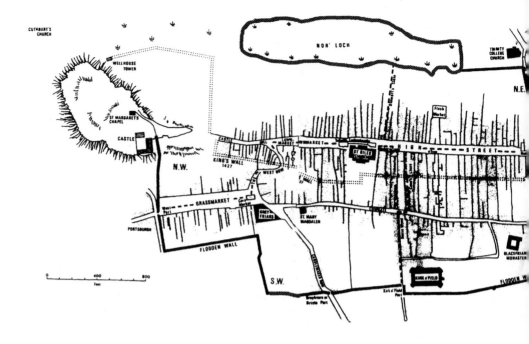

As Provost, Grange added the chief civic position in Edinburgh to his military post as Keeper of the Castle. Edinburgh was the greatest and grandest town in Scotland. A royal borough since the reign of David I, its importance greatly increased in the reign of James III when it became the seat of government and of the supreme courts, as well as the usual residence of the King. By 1478 it was styled a place of opulence. It had grown up in front of the Castle, its High Street, first paved in 1532, extending like a spinal chord from Castlehill down the volcanic ridge to the eastern gateway, the Netherbow Port. The houses on either side were built of unpolished stone, faced with wooden galleries built on the second storey. Here lived the merchants and burgesses. Sir James Mossman, the royal jeweller lived here, and his house, dubbed with the name of John Knox, still stands. On either side of the High Street narrow lanes and closes of tall, densely packed and poorly constructed wooden houses branched out like ribs on the steep slopes descending to the Nor Loch on the north side and to the Grassmarket and Cowgate on the south. In this quarter lived the very poor.[8] A few hundred yards from the Castle stood St Giles, the High Kirk and the dominant building of the capital. No Tolbooth stood in the vicinity of St Giles until 1561 when the new one was built to do service as a gaol, a courthouse and the seat of parliament.

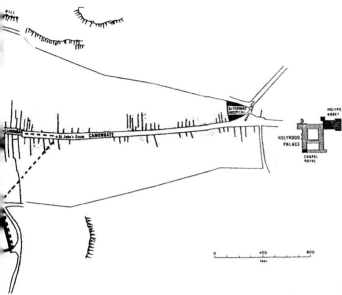

7 Edinburgh, c.1570, from the Castle
to the Canongate.

The Nor Loch (now Princes Street Gardens), constructed by James II,
protected the city on its northern side, although its handsome aspect belied
its main use as a giant cesspit for the city. The same King in 1450 granted the
community the privilege of fortifying the city and surrounding it with a wall.
This hardly seemed of more than symbolic importance until 1513 and the
death of James IV at the battle of Flodden. Early the following year the town
council began the Flodden Wall, of which fragments remain in the south and
south-east, notably along the Pleasance, the Vennel and in the grounds of
George Heriot's School and Greyfriar's churchyard. The wall, built largely of
small unpolished stones, was up to 4 feet in breadth and rising to 24 feet in
height. With rectilinear towers, pierced by dumb bell loops, it provided a
considerable degree of protection, although in places it was not very high and
it could not withstand bombardment. The Burgh was barely 400 yards wide,
the total area within the walls was 140 acres, and its population in 1560 was
in the region of 10,000.[9]

Several 'ports' or fortified gates in the city walls allowed ingress and egress
between dawn and dusk. The West Port, built in 1514 as one of the earliest
security measures taken as a result of the disaster of Flodden, allowed access
from the north and west. The Grassmarket – where cattle and horses were
bought and sold – lay between this gate and the West Bow in the east which

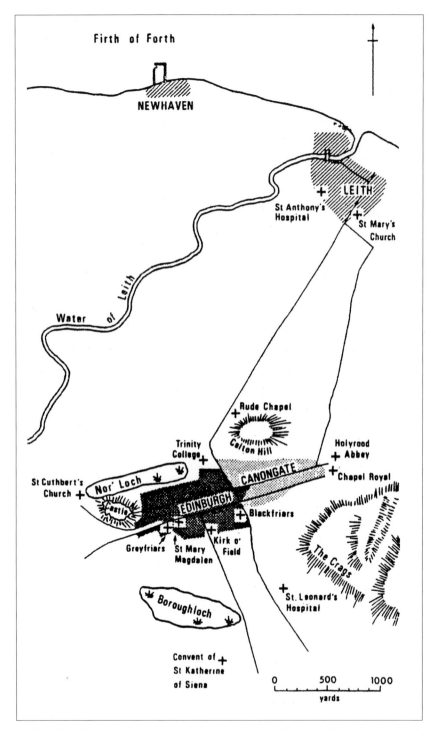

Firth of Forth

NEWHAVEN

LEITH

St Anthony's
Hospital

St Mary's
Church

Water of Leith

Rude Chapel

Calton Hill

Holyrood
Abbey

Trinity
College

CANONGATE

Chapel Royal

St Cuthbert's
Church

Nor' Loch

EDINBURGH

Castle

Blackfriars

Greyfriars   St Mary
Magdalen

Kirk o'
Field

The Crags

Boroughloch

St. Leonard's
Hospital

Convent of
St Katherine
of Siena

0   500   1000

yards

8 Map of Edinburgh, Canongate and Leith, c.1570, showing the Borough loch to the south, and Carlton Hill to the north, the scenes of so many skirmishes.

had its own gate, the Upperbow Port. To the south-east lay the suburb of the Cowgate, once considered the most fashionable part of the town, being the place of residence of the nobility and persons of rank. It lost its allure, when it was enclosed within the city wall on its extension in 1513 and provided with its own gate, the Soo-Gate or Cowgate or Blackfriar's Port, where the Pleasance – named after the Convent of St Mary of Placentia – joined St Mary's Wynd. The lands further south were mostly laid out in gardens belonging to the Dominican monastery of Blackfriars, and the church of St Mary-in-the-Fields, while the grounds further west were in a similar manner laid out by the Franciscan Greyfriars. They too were enclosed and provided with gates: in the vicinity of St Mary-in-the-Field, at the head of the Horse Wynd, was the Kirk o' Field or Potterrow Port, while near Greyfriars stood the Bristo or Greyfriar's Port. The principal gate was the Netherbow Port, a strong twin-towered gatehouse set in a narrow passage between a row of four houses with very thick walls, which stood as a critical defensive feature between the eastern end of High Street and the residential suburb of the Canongate. The first gate had been left in ruins by the English army in 1544 and little repaired, since there seemed no need to defend the borough from its own suburb. The Canongate extended eastwards to Holyrood Palace had its own gates, St Mary's – or the Pleasance Port – to the west and the Watergate to the east. It was a separate ecclesiastical entity with its own Tolbooth, large houses and spacious gardens, and by 1560 had become the preferred abode of the nobility who had decamped from the Cowgate. Leith Wynd was the highroad stretching for two miles from the Netherbow Port to Multries' Hill and then along the line of the present Leith Walk to the fortified seaport of Leith, another independent entity whose sole purpose was to serve – grudgingly – the interests of its great neighbour. It had previously been occupied by Mary of Guise whose French engineers had provided it with impressive state-of the-art defences when she was at war with the Protestants in Edinburgh. Knox described their relationship as 'the auld hatrent.'

Edinburgh was a proud town, and Grange was proud to be its master. He was grateful to Moray for his charge.

2

THE DEVIL'S EGG
August 1567 to January 1570

To do ane horrible and ane unworthy deed
Seek neuer farther than ane Hamilton.
Come neuer a gude bird of the Devil's egg.

The Deploration of the Cruel Murther of James, Earl of Moray.[1]

The new regime was slowly securing itself in a hostile environment. It was not initially recognised by Elizabeth of England – ever fearful of any challenge to the authority of a reigning Queen – let alone by the continental Catholic powers. It was considered to be an illegitimate instrument of usurpation by many in Scotland. It was devoid of the most senior nobility, as Mary's supporters were not slow to emphasise, since, confident that Mary would ultimately be restored, James Hamilton, the Duke of Chatelherault, and the Earls of Huntly and Argyll refused to join the Confederate Lords.[2] The Hamiltons felt particular pique. In their view if there were to be any regent it should be their Duke, a former regent and the heir presumptive to the throne. The Queen's party had among its adherents extreme Reformers such as the Earl of Rothes and conservative Catholics such as Lord Seton. Jacobean attempts to engender dissent and distrust among this unholy alliance of 'Papists' and Protestants 'with no God but gear' by stressing that theirs was the cause of true religion and national survival to which all good Protestants owed allegiance had little effect other than alienating from the King's cause erstwhile adherents. Catholics, such as Eglington and Montrose, who had joined the Protestant Lords to get rid of Bothwell, defected from Moray's camp for a position of uneasy neutrality.

Despite the powerful forces waged against his government, Moray had one initial and enduring advantage, a King regnant and in his clutches, while the

Marians had a Queen who had not only abdicated but was held captive by her enemies. Moray made it clear that he would govern in the King's name and that, if the Hamiltons and their faction would not acknowledge and obey his authority, he would impose it by force.[3] The Hamiltons and their associates were scattered in September, Dunbar, which had stayed loyal to Bothwell, surrendered, and by October Moray could confidently conclude that the realm 'draws to a great quiet and [there is] no appearance of any sturre.'[4] In December this 'godly magistrate' convened his first parliament to confirm the Protestant settlement. Lethington presided. Argyll and Huntly attended. The Regent, despite lack of foreign recognition and in the face of numerical superiority, had triumphed.

Then, suddenly and cataclysmically, the edifice he had constructed was shaken to its foundations. On 2 May 1568 the Queen escaped from Lochleven Castle, sent for Bothwell to return from Denmark, and rushed straight into the arms of the Hamiltons. They were her main strength, but also her Achilles heel since she had to rely on their military competence. Her one remaining fortress was Dumbarton and it was resolved by her party not only to escort her there in force but, by going within striking distance of Moray in Glasgow, to provoke a decisive engagement on home ground. They did, and it was decisive against them. On 13 May 1568 at a village called Langside, Moray and his forces intercepted the Marians and engaged their troops. Grange had hurried from Edinburgh with much of his garrison, and took command of the cavalry. He played a critical role in the battle, his personal bravery and military skill contributing largely to the victory. Moray lost few men and Mary not many more, largely due to her brother's instructions to bring in prisoners and not corpses. But the outcome, though not bloody, proved conclusive. Her hopes crushed, impetuously and fatally Mary fled to England to seek succour from her cousin, Elizabeth. Her cause was immeasurably weakened, out of sight as she was, and in far more secure confinement than Scotland could provide.

Angry that many he had tried to conciliate had eagerly joined in rebellion, Moray at once took action to make such an eventuality impossible again. With 6,000 men and three pieces of small artillery his mobile demolition team destroyed many Marian strongholds in the Borders and overawed the dissident population, but when he ignored the pacific overtures made by Huntly and Argyll, they in turn took up arms and strongly defied him. Huntly plundered Aberdeen and in a daring cavalry raid on Glamis almost seized the Earl of Morton, Moray's main henchman, while Claud Hamilton surprised Hamilton Castle and took it. Meanwhile, in the Queen's name, Athol and Ruthven exacted two months' pay for 200 men out of the burghers of Edinburgh.[5] The

9 A rather insipid portrait of a rather weak man. James Hamilton,
Duke of Chatelherault, *c.*1573.

Marians were doing rather well, until they yielded to pressure from England whose agents were trying to broker a truce. On instruction from Elizabeth they agreed to stay hostilities. Their adversaries were not so forbearing but contemptuously ignored the ceasefire, and held an assembly, dubbed the 'pretended parliament,' to carry out forfeitures against their adversaries. Many of the Queen's party were forfeited, but – on the advice of Lethington and other moderates – not all, since a blanket forfeiture would only increase Marian resistance, or so it was argued.[6] Moray dissolved the parliament and sent forces to Stirling.

It was precisely at this juncture, when his presence was still needed to consolidate his authority in the kingdom, that Moray was constrained to go to England for the York/Westminster Conference which Elizabeth had convened to decide the issue of the validity of Moray's rebellion and that of Mary's complicity in the murder of Darnley. Moray had no choice but to go. Had he refused he would have lost any chance of getting English recognition, and Mary's return would be all the more likely. It was clear, however, that in defending his own actions he would be incriminating his sister. He was accompanied by Morton and Lethington, and brought with him the notorious Casket Letters, the alleged proof of Mary's guilt. Lethington was uneasy about the course Moray was pursuing, and his ready compliance with English demands. He objected to any attempt to try a Scottish monarch in England – it smacked of England's old claim to overlordship. He had acted against his Queen in her own interests, to rescue her from herself, not to depose her. However 'guilty' the Queen might be, her Secretary wanted her restored regardless. By contrast Morton was determined to push the inquiry to its bitter end. How bitter that end could be was made plain in the instructions of the English commissioners: if there were clear evidence of Mary's complicity in the murder of her consort, Elizabeth 'would think her unworthy of a kingdom.' Failing such proof, restored she would be. On 26 November 1568, Moray denounced his sister as a murderer and produced the damning evidence of the Casket Letters. This was the turning point for Lethington who believed that Moray for his own selfish ends had destroyed any prospect of Mary's restoration and endangered the ultimate union of the Crowns by dragging her name through the dirt. A breach was fast becoming a chasm. Elizabeth, however, could not denounce Mary at this juncture for fear of war with Spain. Nor need she – the damage had been done. The English resolved the dilemma by a decision of remarkable dexterity. Accuser and accused were vindicated. Practically things were otherwise. Mary stayed fast in prison, her reputation ruined, while her brother returned home, under English escort through the hostile north, to take up the reins of government, his position enhanced. Elizabeth ordered her Marcher wardens to recognise his regime and only admit Scots bearing the Regent's passport. Two months later she sent Moray a small detachment of troops and some ammunition from Berwick. It was the official end of Scottish isolation.

His return was none too soon. Things had become rather unsettled in Scotland. He had been away too long and his eager dalliance with the English was giving rise to unease among his erstwhile supporters. Things had been calm when the fate of Mary hung in the balance and no one wished to tip it. Now that she was being martyred, reason for restraint had gone. Grange had written anxiously to the Regent warning him of the headway being made by their enemies: 'Huntly reigns in the north, the Hamiltons siege houses and take prisoners, the Hepburns lie in garrison and wait for the Hamiltons to join. Meantime for lack of heads, the willing hearts hang in suspense, whether to abide their fury or to defend themselves.[7]

When Moray reached Edinburgh his sure touch was again rapidly felt, and by early 1569 he was growing in confidence and power while the Marians were again vacillating. He reverted to conciliation since he could not yet afford to break utterly with Lethington, whom he distrusted less than he feared. He galvanised his supporters and ordered a general muster of the kingdom. His determination on the one hand, and tactics on the other, paid off. At Glasgow in March he overawed his southern opponents into concluding an immediate cessation of hostilities, pending a convention of the nobility in April which would settle the affairs of the State and deliberate on the measures to be adopted towards their captive sovereign. Chatelherault and his adherents agreed to acknowledge the authority of the King and the Regent on condition that all those who had been forfeited for their allegiance to the Queen be restored.

When the convention met in Edinburgh, Huntly and Argyll were notably absent and Chatelherault attended a day late and refused to sign the requisite declaration: Mary had begged him not to. It was enough. Moray ordered his arrest. His guards went to the Hamilton lodging in Kirk o' Field Wynd, and there seized the premier peer of Scotland. Along with Lord Herries who had also been arrested, he was imprisoned in Edinburgh Castle, at that time a particularly unsafe lodging as the pestilence had broken out among the garrison.[8] Grange was an indignant gaoler, outraged by what he considered to be a tyrannical breach of trust. His faith in the Regent was shaken.

Argyll and Huntly were now isolated in the north. Moray had out flanked them, was in control of the southern half of the kingdom and was backed by

10 Queen Elizabeth I, *c.*1575, looking more determined
and more intimidating than her rival Mary.

11 The Regent Moray, the 'greatest Captain in the Scottish Israel'.

the power of England. Argyll broke ranks first, and, acknowledging the King's authority, was immediately restored to favour. Huntly, the last of the Queen's lieutenants, finally yielded to the present realities and submitted to the triumphant Regent at St Andrews in May 1569 when he acknowledged the legitimacy of Moray's governance, surrendered his artillery, interceded for his followers and gave hostages for his good conduct. By July, Moray reported to Elizabeth that 'none of the great mass of the North, or very few, are disobedient.' Her agent concurred: 'All is quiet' on the Northern front, 'unless a storm arise from the South.'[9] It did.

In this calm before the storm, the nobility gathered at Perth for another convention to consider Elizabeth's proposals on the disposal of the Marian problem: a confirmation of her abdication, or a restoration to joint sovereignty, or to full sovereignty under safeguards. Her supporters were heavily outnumbered. Huntly was present, but Argyll was not, and Herries and the Duke were otherwise detained. The whole proceedings were a foregone conclusion: the only proposal acceptable to the majority was the first. Lethington 'opposed mightily, and raged, but prevailed not.' A row developed between partisans for both sides, until charges of treason were threatened against any who opposed the King's authority in future.[10] Lethington was permanently alienated from his erstwhile associates and withdrew to Athol, safer among friends.

The increasingly dissentient Secretary was the main problem and greatest danger – even in Athol he could become the focus for all the Marian sympathisers and could give an increased prestige and cohesion to their cause. Moray recognised in Lethington the one man in Scotland equal in capacity to himself. To remove him was to lance the boil of opposition. By deft stage management, he summoned Lethington to court in Stirling on 3 September. Scarcely had he taken his seat in the council than Captain Thomas Crawford of Jordanhill, one of the Earl of Lennox's men, rushed in with a commission from his master, fell to his knees before Moray and demanded justice be done to Lethington and Balfour as the murderers of Darnley. The Regent complied and Lethington was imprisoned in Stirling Castle, complaining that 'a Christian man among the Turks would not have been so cruelly used.'[11] Balfour, despite the amnesty granted him, was arrested at his home.

Lethington thought that he would have been put to death in Stirling had his enemies not thought that by using him as a 'steall guse' – or lure – they could prise the Castle of Edinburgh out of Grange's hands. Grange was suspect and had immediately expressed his anger at this attempt – in blatant breach of trust – to silence the Secretary. It compounded tenfold what had happened to the Duke of Chatelherault. Well aware of Grange's feelings, Moray escorted Lethington to the city and lodged him under guard with David Forrester, one of the Regent's dependants, whose house was on Castlehill just outside the Castle gate. Lord Home and his borderers kept sullen guard. If Moray intended to arrest Grange, or if Morton intended to kill him as Melville alleged, it was not what happened. Grange came to the house that evening, and either by forging the Regent's hand on a warrant, or by connivance with young Lord Home, or by sheer force of personality, got the transfer of the prisoner to his charge, and spirited Lethington away. The bird in the hand had escaped. The next morning Moray came to the Castle, assuring Lethington of his friendship and Grange of his good intentions. Grange gave him the benefit of the doubt since he could easily believe that

12 The prospect of the palace of Linlithgow from the west. It was here that Moray met his end.

the hand behind Lethington's ill-usage was Morton's and not Moray's, and promised to produce Lethington for trial.[12]

When the day arrived, so did a myriad of supporters of the Secretary. Home virtually secured the town with his Border Horse, and Morton refused to enter Edinburgh against such odds. Clement Little, Lethington's advocate, protested that as the prosecutor had failed to appear his client should be acquitted. Moray, who had taken care to be strongly guarded, would not be intimidated. He stood up and declared that as long as the town were occupied by armed troops, no trial should take place and no verdict pronounced. He would continue this day of law another time, and if the accused were found guilty it would not lie in their hands to save him. With those defiant words ringing in their ears he adjourned the hearing and Lethington remained a prisoner in the comfort of the Castle.[13]

The other intractable irritant in the kingdom was Dumbarton Castle. Moray sent forces under the Earls of Mar and Glencairn to seek its surrender or take it by storm. With foresight, Lord Fleming, the Keeper, had increased the security of his charge by hiring up to 100 hagbutters to fortify the parish church and entrench the whole town 'as a fortress.' Town and castle could hold out for some time, time that was needed to allow the expected French aid to arrive. He entered into protracted negotiations. When 'two great ships from France, laden with all manner of victuals,' arrived in Loch Ryan, and under the noses of the Regent's men, disembarked, Fleming, refreshed and replenished, held on.[14]

Moray could not foreclose on Dumbarton in person, since events begun in England demanded his presence in an ever more wobbly capital. In England, although the Northern Rebellion – whose principal aim was to free Mary – had collapsed, its ringleaders – the Earls of Northumberland and Westmorland – were still at large and had sought refuge in the Scottish Borders, an area 'much addicted to the rebels.' The addiction was not shared. 'The vermin are fled to foreign cover,' quipped Cecil. Westmorland was safe with Grange's son-in-law, Kerr of Fernihurst, who refused to hand him over, but on Christmas Day Northumberland was betrayed and taken prisoner to Edinburgh where he was lodged in the house of a burgess – not in the Castle – before being moved to Lochleven. Moray, it was rumoured, would exchange the Earl for Mary. Northumberland's treatment caused outrage throughout Scotland since it was accepted practice that those who escaped across the Border were immune from arrest. Huntly and Argyll were on the verge of revolt, and even Morton was staggered by this move and opposed surrendering the Earl to the English. Grange threatened to release Lethington, Chatelherault and Herries if Moray made any further moves against Northumberland or Westmorland.[15]

Moray, however, would make no more moves against anyone. On 23 January 1570, while passing through the streets of Linlithgow he was assassinated by James Hamilton of Bothwellhaugh acting with the connivance and encouragement of his uncle John Hamilton, Archbishop of St Andrews, from whose house the shot was fired and to whom the assassin fled for succour. The Hamiltons rejoiced in their handiwork, assembled with Argyll in Glasgow and confidently prepared to march on Edinburgh and free their Duke, but the general uprising that they had hoped Moray's assassination would provoke failed to materialise. Grange was outraged by the murder, held Chatelherault more securely than before, and sent word to Fleming to admit no fugitives into Dumbarton. Controversial though Moray's rule was, and his popularity eroded by his deference to England, the manner of his murder and the dignity of his dying brought about an immediate and dramatic rehabilitation. Prior to its internment in St Giles, his body was carried to the Tolbooth in Edinburgh to be put on public display and give vent to demands for revenge. But sorrow was the predominant emotion – and trepidation. 'The death of my Lord Regent,' the *Diurnal* records, 'was the caus of great dolour.' The dolour was not confined to Scotland. A strangely tearful Elizabeth belatedly realised that she had lost her 'best and most useful friend in all the world' and 'the only stay and cause of quietness.'[16] She had, in addition, almost lost Scotland. Troops were sent to the frontier.

The death of Moray was a near fatal disaster for the Jacobean cause and for the kingdom. Moray was in the final stages of defeating the Marian forces and had the stature to bring them back into the fold. He could have reconciled old opponents to necessity, demonstrating that opposition was fruitless and compliance rewarded. Had he lived, Scotland might well have been spared years of bloody civil conflict and an abiding bitterness spanning generations. The Devil's egg brought forth an evil brood.

3

THE SOUL OF ALL
THE GODLESS BAND
February 1570 to March 1571

This blow bred great alteration in the state.
Lord Herries[1]

I am glad to think that Lethington, who is accounted the flower of the
wits in Scotland, shall see himself overmatched.
Elizabeth I[2]

As the son of James IV and the uncle of James VI, Moray had been the obvious
choice for Regent. He had charisma, political acumen and above all, a
legitimacy from his appointment by Mary herself that no other Regent could
possess. Some, such as Grange, were loyal to him personally and would not
consider defecting while he held power. There was no obvious successor and
for five months no one was appointed.

During this vacuum, the 'son's party daily decay[ed].'[3] Only Lennox,
Morton, Mar and Glencairn among the senior nobility adhered to the King's
cause, and even among the lesser grandees support was far from widespread. In
Fife there was Lord Lindsay, and Glammis in Angus. Ruthven, Ochiltree,
Semple and Methven also stayed loyal. The Kirk of course was unshaken and
unshakeable. Popular sentiment in the lowland towns was on their side but, to
the main protagonists, such aid was both fickle and relatively unimportant.
They looked to England for military support and finance, but England seemed
loathe to provide either.

By contrast the Queen's champions were everywhere active and
unchallenged, the 'strongest both among the nobility, gentlemen, and
generally all the land indwellers of shires.' At the fore were the 'petty princes'
– Chatelherault, Argyll, Athol and Huntly. Following them other considerable

Earls – Crawford, Rothes, Errol, Eglinton, Cassilis – and the Lords Herries, Seton, Boyd, Gray, Ogilvie, Fleming, Oliphant and Home. Other prominent supporters were Chatelherault's reckless and wilful sons, James and Claud, the sheriffs of Ayr and Linlithgow, and the lairds of Buccleugh, Fernihurst and Tullibardine. They had the assurance of money from Mary's French dowry, France promised assistance, and Spain favoured them, as did the Pope and loyal Catholics everywhere, especially in England.[4]

They had men, money, land and strongholds: a stranglehold on the country. Where the King's men could boast Stirling and Tantallon, the Queen's possessed 'the chief castles and places of strength', Edinburgh, Lochmaben and Dumbarton, the first commanding the capital of the country, the second dominating the Borders, the third from its situation on the Clyde affording a port and safe haven for foreign ships and succour. The fate of Dumbarton Castle seemed to symbolise the change in fortunes. It was on the verge of surrender when news of the Regent's murder transformed its prospects, since Mar and Glencairn immediately raised the siege and made for Stirling to protect the young King. Dumbarton remained for many more months a persistent thorn in the side of the administration, and provided the rebels with a lifeline to France. Their chief strength, however, lay not in stones but in leaders: Kirkcaldy of Grange and Maitland of Lethington, Grange being universally reputed the bravest and most fortunate soldier and Lethington the ablest statesman in the country, 'himself a host.'[5]

Moray's death had removed the last restraint on both, Lethington having no peer in statecraft now that Moray was gone, Grange having no personal fidelity to any future Regent, least of all one appointed by a small faction and not by the consent of the whole nobility and of the Queen. One last act of respect to his old friend he could pay, and did. On 14 February the state funeral took place. Grange, bearing a pennant displaying the red lion, rode at the head of a solemn procession of the principal Protestant nobility as they carried the bier from Holyrood to the High Kirk of St Giles. Behind them thronged the magistrates and citizens of Edinburgh. Through the great west doors of the church, and up the main aisle Kirkcaldy led the cortege in silence, and slowly lowered the coffin in front of the pulpit for the spiritual leader of the nation to consecrate the passing of its temporal ruler. In his sermon on the text 'Blessed are these that die in the Lord' John Knox, 'with his one foot in the grave'[6] could still move the 3,000-strong congregation to tears for the greatest Captain in the Scottish Israel. In a single solemn ceremony Grange said farewell to his old comrade in arms and to his old allegiance. But he had not yet formed a new one.

IOANNES CNOXVS.

13 The only contemporary portrait of John Knox, from Beza's *Icones*.

The very same day, Maitland of Lethington was also carried through the streets of the capital in his litter from the Castle to the Tolbooth for his trial. Thus from opposite ends of the High Street these two formidable figures, one dead and one 'dying by inches,' made their way to the heart of Edinburgh. A few yards from where Knox had uttered his panegyric for the fallen Regent, the Secretary made a strong speech in his own defence with such effect that even his enemies on the council thought it prudent to adjudge him innocent and set him at liberty, reinstating him to his accustomed office 'as a profitable member of the commonwealth' and one who had been an excellent instrument in 'the forth-setting of God's glory.'[7]

14 Late sixteenth-century iron helmet, of the sort worn at the siege.

The grand old man may have been vindicated and freed, but he was ailing in health, suffering from a creeping paralysis, his ailments being charitably attributed to his recent marriage to Mary Fleming, thirty years his junior: 'To this end hath the blessed joy of a young wife brought him.'[8] His enemies were united in their venom against the chief apostate. To Morton he was the cardinal culprit, 'the whole forthsetter of the other side.' Buchanan denounced him as a 'chameleon, inconsistent and treacherous,' all the more so because of his prodigious ability. And Bannatyne derided him as 'the head of wit, called Michael Wylie with his sore feet.' In March, the English ambassador, Randolph, summed up the general perception that while 'his legs are clean gone, his body so weak he cannot walk, even sneezing is an agony' and 'only his heart and stomach are good,' yet 'his wits are sharp enough.'[9]

Lethington withdrew to his country seat of Lethington to recuperate and plot. His sharp mind was 'more given to policy than to Mr Knox's preaching,' and that policy was to restore the Queen. It is a tribute to the extraordinary character of the man that despite his infirmities, he was quite simply 'the soul of all the godless band' as Calderwood put it. The disaffected came to his door and sat at his feet. 'All this time there was great recourse to Lethington who

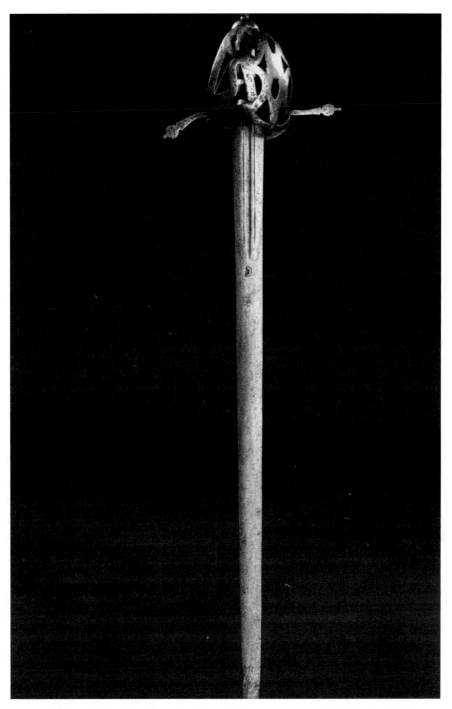

15 Ribbon basket hilted broadsword, with long counter-curved quillons, *c*.1570.

was lying sick of the gut. His house was therefore called the school, he the schoolmaster, and such as repaired to him, his disciples.' 'His head governs Argyll and Huntly and all that gang,' observed Lord Hunsdon, the Governor of Berwick.

In early March the King's faction put an end to their dithering and met in Morton's house in Edinburgh to deliberate on the issue of a successor to Moray as Regent. Such deliberations were beset by difficulties. The Marian position was clear: the Queen's commission was made void by the death of Moray, and they could never approve another Regent ruling on behalf of an infant King, but only royal lieutenants appointed by the Queen to rule at her behest. By contrast the King's party wanted to appoint as Regent Darnley's father, the Earl of Lennox, but were unsure of the constitutional basis on which they could make such an appointment. Some thought that a new election could be made grounded on the original commission, while the more extreme denied that any commission had been necessary, and that the King's party should proceed to an election without delay. That option was not possible, however, since the Jacobeans dared not act until they had Elizabeth's approval of their resolve and of their choice.

England was ever the shadow at the door. Elizabeth was beset by divergent views on how to react to events in Scotland. Morton blew the flame of her anxiety by accounts of the succour given by the Marians to the English rebels, the hostile activity of Lethington, the expected desertion of Grange and the warlike preparations of their opponents. John Gordon, the Marian emissary, on the other hand, warned her not to back one faction in Scotland 'against the rest of the ancient nobility,' but to use her good offices to unite the country. Otherwise her nightmare might come true of the Marian nobles being forced to take up the French offer of men and money.[10] She could not allow those who gave succour to her rebels to triumph, but she feared the vast expense of a campaign in Scotland and the resultant threat of French intervention.

In a quandary Elizabeth counselled suspending the election pending the signing of a peace treaty, but at the same time sent Sussex to the Borders in mid-April to seek for the fugitive English traitors and those who harboured them. Since all of those were Marians her intervention would necessarily buttress the King's party. Over the next few weeks the English forces ravaged the Borders leaving ninety pillaged towns and burnt castles – including Fernihurst – in their wake. Sussex urged Elizabeth to follow up his success by taking sides openly and using his power to conclude the matter quickly and decisively. If she dithered longer the opportunity might be lost for good: 'God put into your heart to choose the most honourable and sure course, for all

Scotland looks to what end your force shall bend... My grandfather charged me never to trust Scot or Frenchman further than I had the surety in my own hands.' With his army poised to invade, she commanded him to arbitrate a concord.[11]

Grange was still not past the Rubicon but he was riding fast in that direction. The English sorties on the Borders and the imminent appointment of the Anglophile Lennox as Regent, aroused his fierce patriotism. England had always been *the* Enemy, France *the* Friend. As a result of the Reformation, for the first time in Scottish history two bad neighbours had become perforce each other's only friend. Grange was a Protestant and knew how essential it was for Scotland and England to end their feuding, but he feared the smaller country losing its soul to the larger, as some of her rapacious nobility had lost theirs to English gold.

Already by the end of April, when he peremptorily refused Morton entry into Edinburgh, it was clear to some observers that Grange 'had clean revolted without any further hope'. Yet a few days later he was writing to Randolph assuring him that he would 'remain... the King's faithful subject and shall maintain his authority... and keep the [Castle] on his behalf.' It is likely that Grange was still wrestling with the conflicting calls on his allegiance and the mixed signals he was sending out were a result of his own genuine internal convulsions. To Cecil, Randolph confessed to finding 'a great spot of dishonesty in Grange.' He had believed him to be – after Moray – the faithfullest friend to England,' but that was before 'he had become enchanted by Lethington.' Randolph would 'not rush to disown' his old friend whom he had known from their student days in Paris, but soon he would either prove himself 'a true man or be shamed forever.'[12] Randolph's forebearance was not widely shared. The almost unanimous view of the King's party and of the English was that Grange, under the malign influence of the Secretary, had already thrown in his lot with the other side.

Randolph's view of Lethington as the eminence grise was reciprocated. The Secretary bypassed the ambassador and corresponded directly with Sussex considering the former an 'evil instrument' since it was his missives, he was sure, that were turning Elizabeth against them. The Queen could not have followed the course she now adopted, if truly informed of the state of Scotland. Sussex, still trying to avoid bloodshed by getting the rival sides to submit to Elizabeth's arbitration, warned the Secretary that if his faction continued in their support of the English rebels and in their opposition to the King's party he would be forced to intervene. Conversely, if they disarmed he would appeal to the rival side to do likewise so that civil war might be averted.

Morton and Mar complained that while Sussex was corresponding with the rebels they were taking advantage of the 'drift of time' to increase their strength.[13]

This analysis was brutally confirmed when on 10 May, in the midst of these negotiations, the recently released Chatelherault, aided by Westmorland and other English rebels, besieged the castle at Glasgow. This flagrant act of aggression and contempt forced Sussex's hand. Lethington, he concluded must be behind it. The Secretary, he had been told, had said that he would make 'Elizabeth sit on her tail and whine like a whipped hound.'[14] It is hard to see Lethington's hand behind this rash action (although he was capable of coarse and injudicious language). Glasgow Castle was hardly a pivotal strategic gain. It was a small Lennox outpost held by James Stewart of Minto with eighteen men, and to besiege it at this juncture could provoke English intervention on the side of the King's party. This was not the work of the canny Secretary but of those unsubtle jackals, the Hamiltons, once more bent on petty revenge and to hell with the cost. Costly it was.

On Thursday 11 May 1570 over 1,000 infantry, 400 cavalry, and four field culverins, under the command of the deputy governor of Berwick, William Drury, were sent into Scotland. Lennox accompanied them. They reached Edinburgh two days later and rested. No siege was contemplated since the English had not brought with them the sort of ordnance needed to reduce so strong a castle. Their professed mission was not to 'intermeddle' in Scottish affairs but only 'to pursue the Queen's rebels and' – ominously – 'their favourers.'[15] Sussex, however, was clear that his intervention was crucial to the survival of the King's party and to thwart French ambitions in Scotland, and that it was only just in time. While the English tried to persuade Lethington and Grange to come to heel on Elizabeth's terms, they were subjected to traditional Scots' hospitality, several soldiers being beaten up in drunken brawls and their horses stolen.[16]

Three days later the army marched towards Glasgow, joined with Morton's men from Stirling, and prepared for a pincer movement on the rebels. The effect of the approach of this combined force was to disperse those besieging the castle. Some retired to Dumbarton, some to Hamilton, the rest to the north. To punish the Duke the allied army then laid siege to Hamilton Castle. It was stoutly defended until two culverins brought from Stirling were planted in battery. Recognising the inevitable the garrison surrendered, the castle was blown up, the town was burnt, and the palace was demolished. A similar fate befell several other Hamilton seats in Clydesdale.[17]

Dumbarton Castle remained the outstanding irritant, 'the only place in the realm that remained disobedient to the King.' Drury decided to see if he could

16 Sir William Drury, the English general.

talk the garrison into surrender and sent a placatory message to Lord Fleming
eliciting an offer for a meeting at the village of Kilpatrick, half-way between
Glasgow and Dumbarton. When Drury arrived at the appointed time he
found no one there. He proceeded to ride on to Dumbarton some five miles
away, sending word of his coming. The reply he received was that he should
approach the castle with one or two men, but when he got within firing range
Fleming declined to come out. As Drury turned his horse a falcon was
discharged and rounds from a harquebus were fired from the ramparts. He
escaped the gunshot, unscathed but incandescent, and was making his way
back when a large party of Fleming's men came in pursuit. There was a brief
but violent altercation in which two men from the castle fell to their deaths on
the rocks, and one was slain and transported back to Dumbarton on a

17 The Regent Lennox with his Countess, Lady Margaret Douglas,
and his younger son, Lord Charles Stewart.

makeshift stretcher of harquebus barrels. Drury suffered just one man
wounded.[18]

The effect of this dishonourable behaviour was immediate. Sussex and
Lennox both implored Cecil to authorise a major campaign to take Edinburgh
and Dumbarton Castles and to reduce the rebels to submission. So real seemed
the threat that Lethington 'took his flight from the Castle of Edinburgh, and
lighted at length in the Blair of Athol.'[19] But Elizabeth was not so sanguine –
or foolhardy – as her generals and would not countenance a siege of either
citadel. The expense and logistics of such operations would be formidable and
she evinced her usual reluctance to commit herself to such endeavours. She had

done enough, and it had cost enough – nearly £17,000 – already. She was also aware that Charles IX of France had begun to muster troops to send to Scotland. She ordered a withdrawal and further allayed French fears by urging their King to send an emissary to help negotiate a truce in Scotland.[20] On 1 June the English departed for Berwick, leaving their placeman as Regent-designate.

The King's party could wait no longer for a leader. Matthew Stewart, Earl of Lennox, duly became Regent on 17 July 1570 at a convention held in the Edinburgh Tolbooth. He was, as the King's grandfather and nearest adult male relative, the natural choice, but southern support and the gold that accompanied it clinched the matter. Lennox was Elizabeth's creature, and her patronage alienated further those who feared English hegemony and favoured Mary's restoration as a bulwark against it. Even his backers did not like the man. He was taciturn, dour, suspicious and with a bad reputation for being a bully when he had the upper hand. Only Morton was staunch in support but it was support without liking or respect.[21] Mary had acquiesced in Moray's appointment: Lennox had no such sanction. For the Marians he was not Regent of the nation but the representative of a party within the nation. Lethington stayed away from a ceremony whose legitimacy he could not accept, and Grange, never one to disguise his antipathy for Lennox, treated the whole proceedings with contempt. He refused to be present and ordered that no cannon should be fired after the proclamation. Although Grange stood aloof from Lennox and his supporters, he had not, in his own mind at least, committed himself irrevocably to the Marians, and Randolph still wavered in his assessment of him. Not for long. A few days later Grange again defied the new Regent when Lennox ordered him to send him some field pieces from the Castle's arsenal. Knowing how they would be used, he refused, asserting that he would be 'a procurer of peace and not an instrument of war, and shedding of Scottish blood.'[22] This refusal finally convinced the English ambassador that Grange was now committed to the Marian cause and that civil war was inevitable.

Practising 'his old craft,' Lethington determined to create an alternative administration to that of Lennox. To that end he summoned a rival parliament to meet at Linlithgow in August, and he entered into correspondence with the Duke of Alva in Flanders, Charles IX in France and Mary in England. The French King promised to give the Queen's party help to keep the castles of Edinburgh and Dumbarton, and sent his *valet de chambre*, Monsieur Verac, as his agent to Scotland to work for the Auld Alliance and to advance the Queen's cause. He was to be the harbinger of more ample and tangible support, and should it arrive the Regent's tenure in office would be short. In

Edinburgh rumours of Mary's imminent return were 'as common as meal in the market,' and others – of an invasion by Alva or of a plot by Grange to hang the leading burgesses – circulated. In an attempt to disrupt Lethington's machinations the authorities in Berwick were put on alert to apprehend his principal agent, Thomas Cowie, 'a very young man, of slender body, evil face and little beard,' and Sussex warned Lethington that he would not 'suffer the King's nobles to be suppressed.'[23]

Military counters to the new Regent went ahead regardless. Chatelherault mustered in the south-west; Argyll and his men made ready to ravage the lowlands; and Huntly assembled his forces at Brechin. While their forces were still split Lennox and Morton acted with the vigour of the desperate and managed to levy some 7,000 men to march against the weakest link. It snapped on impact. On 11 August they stormed Brechin and strung up the garrison before Huntly's own house, the first example of a brutality that was to be much followed in the days to come.[24] Huntly took to the hills. In rapid succession Lethington and his two brothers were put to the horn and their lands seized, Robert Pitcairn, the Commendator of Dunfermline, displaced Lethington as Secretary, and Chatelherault and his sons were outlawed.

In Edinburgh James McGill was elected Provost and Morton made sheriff principal. Hemmed in, Grange increased the Castle garrison, continued with further fortification, and replenished his supplies. The bakers were forced to work day and night baking biscuit. He bought all the butter and cheese in the market and paid for it with good French crowns. He also consulted the craft deacons to find out how they would react to a siege of the Castle by the English. Their answer was little to his liking: they would give Grange such assistance as the Regent authorised. A rumour soon spread that Grange and his allies intended to seize the town by subterfuge and hang the principal citizens in their own stairwells. Panic swept the streets and all householders were ordered on pain of death to report to the town council any armed strangers lodging with them. Yet aspects of normality continued amidst the troubles: there was time to perform the ritual of half-drowning and then burning John Swan and John Listar on Castlehill for sodomy, time to burn a brother and sister for having 'carnal copulation together,' time to hang the minister of Spott for murdering his wife, and time to record these events in considerable detail for the edification of posterity.[25]

Lennox was impotent against the might of the castle. He could, however, exact vengeance on his most bitter foes. Captain David Home raided Lethington to burn the crops and seize the goods. Cunningham and Crawford were sent to the Hamilton lands to destroy 'without commiseration or pity' the property of those who assisted the Queen. Acting on their orders, the captains led a night raid from Glasgow on the tenants and inhabitants of Bothwell Moor, and brought to Edinburgh 400 cattle, 600 sheep and 60 horses. It was hard at times to distinguish military necessity from mere plunder and the distinction was lost on the poor who suffered. They petitioned the Regent directly and persuaded the assistant minister of St Giles, John Craig, to take up their cause. Reluctantly Lennox offered to return half of what was left after the best had already been sold. The losers could either agree to this in full settlement or get nothing.[26] These displays of personal vendetta displeased the English, threatening as they did the peace overtures being pursued by them. In October, Sussex stepped in decisively. He proposed a formal truce during which all forfeited property would be restored to the Marians and all legal proceedings would be administered in the King's name alone. This cessation of hostilities would be, he hoped, a prelude to a permanent peace treaty. This it did not prove to be, but the armistice tottered on until the end of the following March.

Rather disingenuously Sir James Melville, Grange's kinsman, accused the English of trying to foment trouble rather than assuaging it, and ascribed the most nefarious role in the civil war that beset Scotland to their ambassador, Thomas Randolph, himself. According to Melville, once he had split and polarised the parties Randolph fanned the flames, 'knowing by his long residence in Scotland how to play on their weaknesses and enmities.' He was not above bribery; the nobles were not beneath it.

Then as Nero stood up upon a high part of Rome to see the town burning which he had caused set on fire, so master Randolph delighted to see such fire kindled in Scotland, and by his writing to some in the court of England, glorified himself to have brought it to pass in such sort, that it should not be got easily slokenit [extinguished with water] again.[27]

This fanciful and Machiavellian view of the English involvement in Scottish affairs is belied by the records they kept, and the interminable series of negotiations they encouraged.

Grange during this lull could not stand back much longer, sullen, disaffected, but inactive. The divisions were too great, peace between the parties was obviously failing to take hold, and ultimately he had to take sides. It was an incident which impinged on him personally that finally and irrevocably alienated Grange from his erstwhile Protestant associates. In December 1570 John Kirkcaldy, Grange's cousin, was attacked in Dunfermline by the Dury brothers, and their servant Henry Seton. They had drawn their swords on him and, but for the intervention of the provost, would have killed him. A couple of weeks later on 21 December Henry Seton compounded his offence by ridiculing one of Grange's servants. Grange sent six others to give him a good beating. They cornered him with their cudgels on the harbour at Leith. Seton, however, 'being unpatient to be dung as a dog,' drew his sword and wounded one of his assailants. They drew in turn but he managed to hold them off until he was thrown off-balance when he tripped over an anchor cable. Once down he was quickly butchered. Knowing that as a result of the commotion the town guard was on their tracks, the killers made their way back to Grange by crossing the frozen Nor Loch under the protecting guns of the Castle above. All made it to safety, but for one, James Fleming, who was caught and imprisoned in the Edinburgh Tolbooth. Under cover of darkness, Grange sent from the Castle a heavily-armed rescue party who silenced the bell of St Giles, broke open the Tolbooth with a battering ram and liberated the young Fleming. They returned in triumph to a defiant salvo from nine guns of the Spur battery. One shot hit a house near to where Lennox was lodging 'to give defiance to the Regent in his face,' and a barn in the Canongate was damaged. Both the Regent and the Town council, severely embarrassed by this brazen act and their inability to do anything about it, passed it over in silence.[28]

One man, however, would not keep silent, and he had the loudest voice in Edinburgh. On Christmas Eve 1570, from the pulpit of St Giles, John Knox condemned his old friend's actions which were all the blacker for proceeding from a man of such stature.

> Had the perpetrator been a man without God, a throat-cutter and a murderer, one that had never known the works of God, it would have moved me no more than the other riots and enormities which my eyes have seen... But to see the stars fall from heaven, and a man of knowledge commit so manifest a treason what godly heart could not but lament, tremble and fear?

The offending phrase 'murderer and throat-cutter' was related to Grange out of context by someone fishing in troubled waters – so like newspaper reporting in our own times. He immediately wrote to Knox's colleague, Craig, denying he had any part in murder 'for I take God to be my damnation,' and demanding that his character be vindicated as publicly as it had been traduced.[29] Craig wisely procrastinated, saying that he could do nothing without the consent of the Kirk Session, and to them Grange accordingly complained. The session passed his letter onto Knox. Realising his words had been misrepresented, Knox embraced the first opportunity of explaining and vindicating them from the pulpit. He had not called Grange a throat-cutter. The outrage to justice was all the more abhorrent because it was committed not by a murderer but by an erstwhile virtuous man. 'To see men who have felt God's judgement as mercies, and of whom all godly hearts have had a good opinion – to see, I say, such men so far carried away, that both God and man are not only forgot, but also publicly despised, is both dolorous and fearful to be remembered.'[30] Grange dropped his complaint under the impression that Knox had recanted. He could not have been more wrong. The explanation merely damned Grange the more.

The following Sunday, 7 January 1571, when Grange came down to St Giles accompanied by an armed retinue which included those involved in Seaton's death and Fleming's rescue, Knox would not be cowed and warned his hearers against relying on the mercy of God while breaking His commandments 'and proudly defending such transgression.' Grange, further incensed by words he knew directed at him, was heard to mutter threats against the preacher, and when placards were affixed to the church doors, accusing Knox of seditious railings against the sovereign, refusing to pray for her and representing her as a hopeless reprobate, rumours spread that the Governor was become the sworn enemy of Knox and intended to kill him. Several of Knox's leading supporters wrote to Grange warning him against doing anything against that man whom 'God had made the first planter and chief waterer of his church among them.' His death and life were as dear to them as their own.[31] They meant it and they spoke for many others, great and small, in Scotland. By reacting so violently to a personal slight, and by appearing to threaten the very icon of the emergent Protestant nation, Grange had damaged his own position and that of the Marian party in general.

When the General Assembly of the Kirk met in March in the Nether Counsel House, Grange put on a noisy war game, or 'counterfeit skirmish,' on Castlehill, which proclaimed to all where the Keeper's ultimate allegiance lay. He divided his troops in two, one half defending the Castle and the other half playing the English besiegers. The defenders shouted defiance and poured scorn on the attackers: 'Dirt in your teeth!' they cried, 'Hence knaves! And go tell that whore your mistress, ye shall not come here. We let you know we have men, meat, and ordnance for seven years.' At the end of eight hours, with the discharge of three cannon those playing the English took flight. Wishful thinking! Knox bitterly – and presciently – commented: '*Ante ruinam praet fastus*, as saith Solomon, before destruction goeth pride.'[32]

4

DUMBARTON ROCK
1 and 2 April 1571

'[Verac] brought some oranges, some raisins, some biscuit bread, some
powder, some bullet, and... a malediction to furnish Dumbarton'[1]

Cresce diu felix arbor, semperque vireto Frondibus, ut nobis talia poma feras.
[Forever flourish, happy tree, and always bear lush foliage, that you may
again produce such fruit for us.]
Epitaph on the gibbet of the Archbishop of St Andrews[2]

The first 'destruction' was soon in coming. This was the dramatic capture of
the formidable Dumbarton Castle by Captain Thomas Crawford of Jordanhill,
on 2 April 1571.

The name Dumbarton is a corruption of *Dun Breatann*, meaning 'fortress of
the Britons,' the aptly-named ancient stronghold of the Kings of Strathclyde.
Situated on a precipitous rock split into two summits which rose abruptly from
the Clyde at its confluence with the little River Leven, it commanded the sea
lanes entering the Clyde and dominated the surrounding alluvial plain. To its
natural advantages were added strong fortifications. The Over Bailey was
constructed on the level ground between the two summits and extended onto the
eastern lower summit or Beak, while the Nether Bailey was built towards the foot
of the steep southern slope which descended towards the Clyde. The two bailies
were divided by two barriers built across the steep southern defile. The lower
barrier was referred to as the 'chamber between the craggs' the upper barrier was
the Portcullis gate. The southern defile and its entrance gate was further secured at
its mouth by a tower known as the Windy Hall. The Wallace Tower defended the
northern entrance and the White tower, perched on the higher, western summit,
kept watch over the surrounding countryside and the sea. These defences and its

18 Dumbarton in 1690 from the north-west or town-side, showing the Wallace Tower in the centre and the White Tower on the tall crag on the right. The Beak is the smaller summit on the left. An ascent on the far left (or north-east side) of the Beak would not be seen by guards in either tower.

location on a rock with its own water source and joined to the mainland only by a narrow strip of marsh rendered the castle virtually impregnable to all adversaries. Famine or by surprise were the only ways of taking it. Ominously, surprise had done just that when in January 1514 the third Earl of Lennox burrowed under the north gate and captured the castle.

It was of vital strategic importance to the Marians, constituting a considerable menace at the very heart of Lennox country and a focal point of resistance to successive Regents. John, fifth Lord Fleming, had been Keeper since 1565 and had time enough to render his position unassailable by first fortifying the town, and later demolishing the houses of those burgesses who supported the King and taking the stones up to the castle to improve its defences. From this sanctuary Fleming's men scavenged the countryside, despoiling the locals of their goods and maintaining a constant threat on the western flank of the King's supporters. Its position on the Clyde estuary rendered it accessible to foreign ships which brought supplies and, potentially, troops from France. The route from France to the west of Scotland was longer by far than to the east coast, but Leith was out of bounds and the western seaboard far safer from English ships. Once landed, the goods or troops were in the heart of the country and on a navigable river, well protected by the guns and garrison of an imposing stronghold under a loyal and resolute commander. With two pinnaces, its Keeper said, he could control the river and send regular messages to France.[3] Fleming boasted that he had in his hands the 'fetters of Scotland' and whenever the French King had leisure and rest from other wars,

19 Dumbarton from the south-east, or the Clyde-side, showing the Nether Baillie and the Chamber between the Craggs.

if some small force were granted him, he would bring the whole country under their subjection. This was no idle threat.

The French King fed his humour and sent Verac – decried by the Jacobeans as 'a notable pirate' – with some artillery and munitions, and commanded him to stay there and to observe how Scottish affairs went.[4] Lennox feared that Fleming himself would then depart for France to solicit a greater contribution by the French. To prevent this it was absolutely vital that the castle be captured. Previous siege attempts had failed. To take it conventionally would require help from his patron, Elizabeth, in the shape of ships, men and cannon. Such help was not readily forthcoming. Needs must – a plot was hatched which was so audacious as to be almost inconceivable.

Fleming had been lulled into a false sense of security, emboldened by the defection of Edinburgh Castle and the temporary incapacity of the Regent who had not only been injured by a fall from his horse but was in agony from gout. In any case Dumbarton's garrison could relax since the truce precluded military action before April. It was the perfect opportunity for a surprise strike. On 1 April 1571, immediately the truce expired, a raiding party had been assembled in Glasgow under the command of Thomas Crawford of Jordanhill, as brave and skilful a soldier as any in Scotland. His own account is the best source of his most daring escapade.[5] He had soon recognised that the only way to take the castle was by subterfuge, and secured the assistance of a man called Robertson, a former watchman in the castle who knew every inch of it, and the way in which it was garrisoned and guarded. He bore a grudge against Fleming, and for a bribe he consented to guide their way. Crawford's planning was meticulous. A detachment of light horse under John

Cunningham, Laird of Drumwhistle, secured all routes between Dumbarton and Glasgow to prevent word getting back to the garrison. None did. In the evening before its fall many of the castle guard were 'deboshing' – whoring and drinking – in the town of Dumbarton, as had become their wont.[6] At dusk Crawford marched from Glasgow and at about midnight arrived at Dumbuck, a mile from Dumbarton, where he was joined by Cunningham and Captain Home and their men. The horsemen remained where they were, waiting on events. The footmen advanced in silence and single file carrying scaling ladders and grappling irons attached to ropes, their hackbuts on their backs. The whole company was connected with a rope so that none could get lost in the darkness.

They had many ditches to cross and one stretch of deep water – Gruggie's burn – before they reached the castle. As they approached the tree bridge over the burn they were startled by a bright light behind them which they feared were beacons descrying their coming. It was a chimera. When a few retraced their steps the light had vanished. On they went. The summit was shrouded in fog but the base was clear. They chose to scale the Beak, 120 feet above them on the north-east face, far from the entrance gates and their respective towers, and out of sight of any vigilant watchman on the White Tower. It was an inaccessible spot but one where the chance of being caught by a sentry was slight. Their first attempt almost ended in disaster when the ladders lost their hold on the sheer rock face while soldiers were upon them. A vigilant watch would have heard the clamour below and the attempt would have been discovered and repelled. They paused in silence but all was still. Again their ladders were fixed and this time the grappling irons found a secure perch in the crevices of the rock. Their ladders were too short to reach a small jutting-out ledge half-way up the escarpment. Robertson and Crawford climbed the interval and reached the ledge. There an ash tree had struck its roots. The scaling party fastened the ropes to the tree trunk and let them down to the men on the ladders who then hoisted themselves up. When they were all assembled at the tree, they were still far from the foot of the wall. Day was breaking. They managed to place their ladders but were further impeded when one of the men had a panic attack and could go neither further up the ladder nor descend. His hands were glued to the rungs. Crawford ordered the ladder to be turned over and the rest of the party scaled the steps over the rigid body of their comrade.[7]

In this manner they gained the bottom of the wall but the footing was narrow and dangerous. Once more fixing their ladders in the copestone, Alexander Ramsay, Crawford's ensign, and two others, Harry Wetherbourne and George Dundas, stole up, scaled the wall and slew the sentry – who vainly tried to fend them off by throwing stones. His dying cries, however, at last alerted the garrison.

20 George Buchanan, serious and sanctimonious, in 1581.

Crawford and the others surmounted the wall. The weight of those scaling it partly brought down this wall and through the breach came the remaining attackers. Crawford and Home and their men rushed in shouting 'A Darnley! a Darnley!', Crawford's battle-cry, and slew three more of the garrison, who were running about naked and half-asleep. The light mist added to the confusion. Despite their surprise some of the garrison still held the Wallace and White Towers, the Windy Hall, the 'chamber between the crags' and the Nether Baillie. To no avail – their spirit was broken. When Crawford ordered his men to turn the castle ordnance on the defenders, faced with imminent destruction the remnant yielded without a fight, some escaping in the mist.

Fleming was one. He managed to escape down the face of an almost perpendicular cleft in the rock and out of a postern gate which opened on the Clyde. Commandeering a passing fishing boat he and five of his men made their way to Argyllshire, leaving his wife and only son, John, to be taken prisoner. The victors had lost not a man and of the garrison only four were killed. A considerable quantity of money and plate, and ordnance and munitions was seized, the latter all the more vital now that they were starved of all that Edinburgh Castle contained. Also found were 300 hosts, Mass books and vestments.[8] These were destined for the fire. But more important than this booty was the capture of a rare prize, John Hamilton, the infamous Archbishop of St Andrews. He was found in the Wallace Tower with a mail shirt and steel cap on. Calderwood, in a rare shaft of praise, observed that 'had his military companions been equally alert and prepared, the capture of the castle would have been a hopeless undertaking.'[9] Verac was also taken, as was an escaped Northern rebel, whom the Scots handed over to their English allies to deal with.

About noon the Regent arrived to gloat over his great prize and bestow benefactions. Cunningham was made captain of the castle. Crawford was given lands belonging to the archbishop of Glasgow. Magnanimity was shown to Lady Fleming whom Lennox released and to whom he returned her jewels.[10] Her son, however, was kept in prison. Nor did Verac benefit from any immunity when his piratical tendencies were considered to have overtaken his diplomatic ones. He was held in custody for robbing the merchants in the Firth of Clyde, before being returned to France.

The fate of the Archbishop was unhappiest of all. He was taken in triumph to Stirling and imprisoned in the castle. His trial and execution were carried out with great expedition to forestall any intervention by Elizabeth. On 7 April he was arraigned by Ruthven the Justice Clerk, and Buchanan, on charges of being party to the murders of Darnley and Moray, and conspiring to kill Lennox. He denied them all and was duly convicted. Judgement was not long delayed. Sometime after 5 p.m. he was brought in his full episcopal vestments to the gallows at the Mercat Cross of Stirling. On the gibbet he admitted and repented of his involvement in the murder of Moray, but not the other charges. As the bell struck six in the evening, ignominiously to the jeers of the townsfolk, the Archbishop of St Andrews was slowly hanged, after which his body was cut down and dismembered.

The fall of Dumbarton was the death not just of an errant archbishop but of any further hope of foreign aid. The Queen's men, starved of funds and resources and exhausted by continuous struggle were severely weakened. It was quite simply the most serious disaster that could befall the Marian cause other than the fall of Edinburgh Castle itself.

5

CAPTAIN OF THE CRAG
April to May 1571

This hauld it sall me keip
My realm and Princes libertie
Thairin I sall defend,
When traitouris salbe hangit hie,
Or make some schaful end.
Ane Ballat of ye Captane of the Castell[1]

He was humble, gentle, and meek like a lamb in the home but a lion in
the field; a lusty, stark, and well-proportioned personage and of a hardy
and magnanimous courage.
Sir James Melville on Kirkcaldy of Grange[2]

The capture of Dumbarton was so unexpected and shocking that for some time
both sides refused to believe either their respective luck or misfortune. The bishops
of Ross and Galloway, the latter a scion of the Gordon family lately installed in St
Giles as a replacement for Knox, protested that it was Dunbar and not Dumbarton
that had fallen. When the reports were confirmed by Fleming himself, who in
disguise got into Edinburgh Castle on 5 April, the rebels knew that this set-back
had to be countered at once. The Duke, Huntly and Argyll wrote to the King of
France all declaring that there was no discouragement to be taken from this
'tynesyll' [loss]. Nonetheless their reassurances were accompanied by even more
persistent demands for money and men. Lethington later acknowledged that 'the
taking and detaining of Dumbarton... put us in a great strait and the cause in peril
of overthrow, if God had not moved us to prevent the danger with diligence.'[3]

   Grange, determined not to let Lennox triumph, was the first to 'prevent the
danger' by finally and irrevocably throwing in his lot with the Marians. His

21 The swashbuckling Lord Claud Hamilton.

defection with the Castle he held seemed destined to prolong indefinitely the increasingly bitter struggle, and the concomitant suffering of the nation. Calderwood denigrated the apostate: 'Now is seen that which men would scarcely have believed before: the Laird of Grange joining with the Hamiltons, who slew his master.' It was to this resort that his antipathy to Lennox had propelled him. With his habitual energy Grange immediately took measures to ensure that

22 The High Kirk of
St Giles.

the fate of Dumbarton would not befall the last bastion where Mary's banner flew.
He rendered the Castle as defensible as possible by repairing the walls wherever they
were decayed, cutting away all the prominences which might have assisted any
attempt to scale the rocks, and carefully scarping and smoothing the bank under the
guns of the Spur with the same intent. Surprise was what he feared most, not
bombardment, since the only siege guns in Scotland capable of reducing Edinburgh
Castle lay within that self-same Castle. Nonetheless, he took all of the town's
ordnance inside the citadel and dispatched his brother James to France to bring back
more guns and munitions. With his protégé firmly in command of the greatest
fortress of the kingdom, there was every reason for Lethington, infirm in body as
he was, to return to the heart of things for his grand finale. He came to Leith by
boat at night and had to be carried up to the Castle by six workmen with 'sting and
ling' – by poles in litter-fashion – with Robert Maitland holding his head.[4]

The town of Edinburgh also had to be secured. The Queen's lords rallied in
support. On 14 April, Herries and Maxwell rushed to the capital with 240

horse, and Fernihurst soon followed. Claud Hamilton arrived six days later and Argyll and Boyd came too. In addition to their own retainers the Marian lords paid for 100 mounted lancers and 500 foot soldiers, under the command of Captains Bruce, Hamilton, Melville, Montgomerie and Lauder – who was also sergeant major of the town's militia. Grange had the recruiting drum beaten through the streets and offered a down payment of wages in good French gold to those who mustered at the Castlehill, a tempting offer to many an artisan. Some of Grange's men occupied Holyrood Palace and others strengthened the steeple of St Giles to receive a gun battery on the stone bartizan, beneath the flying arches of the imperial crown that surmounts the tower. The town walls were hastily repaired and half of the Netherbow was closed up. The city was effectively under martial law. On 16 April an English agent, William Herle, reported to Burghley that the town was in Grange's hands.[5]

Some of the residents actively favoured the Marians, others were prepared to live – and trade – with them, and during his occupation Grange was supplied by three apothecaries, three candlemakers, six maltmen, four bakers, nine tailors and clothiers, two shoemakers, three skinners, two smiths and two goldsmiths.[6] Despite the obvious disincentives, many of the leading townsfolk favoured the Regent's party. Dissent had to be suppressed. Captain Melville searched the house of Robert Lekprevik, the Protestant printer, for a scurrilous tract by Buchanan called *The Chameleon* or *Crafty Statesman* in which all Lethington's 'practices and pageants were lively expressed.' The printer had been warned of his approach and escaped in the nick of time, carrying off or burning any incriminating documents. James Inglis, an influential baillie and a staunch King's man, was arrested and imprisoned in the Castle. Grange's worst suspicions were confirmed by the seizure of the Provost, James McGill, and eight burgesses, all fully armed and with a stash of weapons hidden in the Tolbooth. A round-up of suspects was ordered and peremptorily carried out. Captain Melville and his men barged into Andrew Henderson's house in the early hours of the morning and seized him, four of McGill's servants and two young scholars from St Andrews. When his wife protested at their behaviour, one of the soldiers struck her so hard that she died. Bully-boy tactics could backfire. One night four youngsters gave cheek to the steeple guard, bidding them 'remember Brechin' and then slipped away. When the steeple guard came down they encountered the cross-guard and, mistaking them for the miscreants, set upon them. Eight or nine soldiers were badly hurt, some even mutilated, and the following morning their blood was still to be seen on the streets.[7]

It was vital that the Regent regained control of the capital. Morton was the enforcer and his muster point was his castle, the dreaded Lion's Den, at

Dalkeith. The first exchange of fire between the rival forces took place on Sunday 29 April at the Netherbow Port. Morton had sent a company of seventy horse and 100 hagbuteers to Leith to protect the royal herald while he was making a proclamation forbidding all trade with Edinburgh. On their way back to Dalkeith they went up Leith Wynd and took the opportunity to fire their hagbuts into the Netherbow for a space of half an hour, causing panic among the civilian populace. Hearing the uproar, Grange rapidly mustered a force of nearly 300 pike men and harquebusiers who issued out of the Kirk o' Field Port in pursuit. The two sides came to blows at a part of the Boroughmuir called the Powburne. Morton's troops, though outnumbered and under fire from the Castle, got the better of their assailants who were so closely chased back inside the walls that their officer Captain Moffat was speared while he was shutting the gate. Several were killed and wounded on both sides. This 'first yoking', called the Lowsie-Law because it was fought near to a little hill (or law) where the beggars used to sun and louse themselves, marked the beginning of 'the wars between Leith and Edinburgh.'[8]

The following day Grange commanded all the Regent's supporters to leave the town within six hours. The Tolbooth and the house of its Keeper, Andrew Lindsay, were occupied and the resident scribes forced to move after handing over the parliament records. By contrast, the three clerks of the Court of Session were forbidden to leave the Burgh. Lethington boasted that the King's lords would find it difficult to re-establish the court, as the clerks, papers and processes were all held in Edinburgh. The result 'would be a great hinder to their authority.'[9] No records of the Burgh Council exist for the period from 1 May 1571 to 13 November 1573, an indication of the civic disruption at the time. The Regent's house was looted and beds and other movables taken away. The keys of the town were seized from the baillies, and all gates were closed except the Netherbow and West Ports. Pulling down of houses near the Netherbow to improve the town's defences began, and to defend the Castle the construction of a buttress above the Butter Tron and another at the Wester Boll was started. Further defensive work on the strategically-situated St Giles was undertaken, this time on the structure itself. Holes were made in the vault through which guns could be fired at any who entered or attacked the kirk. Other loopholes allowed snipers to command the churchyard to the south, the Lawnmarket to the west and the High Street eastward. Lifelines with the outside world were vital. Supplies could get through if there was sufficient military presence. A contingent of horse and foot had to be sent down to Leith to bring up the provisions which James Kirkcaldy had brought from France in a barque. Selling some of the Queen's jewels to finance his purchases, he had bought munitions, some small ordnance, food and money. The escort brought up six coffers supposedly filled with gold and made out they had enough to pay 1,000 men for a year.[10]

In this feverish atmosphere, and with the Hamiltons back in town, Knox's friends feared for the preacher's safety. He had already been subjected to one assassination attempt when a shot had been fired through his window and even St Giles was no longer safe since the holes made in the roof could easily be utilised by a sniper. They watched over his house and proposed to form a guard when he went to church. Grange forbade the formation of such an escort as casting aspersions on his intentions, and offered instead to house Knox in the Castle and allocate Captain David Melville, his own uncle, to conduct the preacher to and from church. Bannatyne wryly commented that 'he would give the wolf the wedder to keep.' Knox declined the offer. The arrival of Chatelherault on 4 May with a further 100 horse and seventy hagbuteers increased the sense of unease. Grange, his anger cooled and obviously anxious to make amends to his old friend, applied to the Duke for a safe-conduct for Knox but this was refused on the grounds that the reformer had so many enemies that other rascals might do him harm without their knowledge. When this refusal and its reason became known, the elders of the Kirk and John Craig himself came to exert moral blackmail. They warned Knox that to defend him they would be putting their own lives at risk, and after persistent cajoling he agreed to remove himself from the city, for their sakes, and 'sore against his will.'[11]

On 5 May the old preacher left Edinburgh for the security of St Andrews. His fears were soon shown to be only too well justified. An inhabitant of Leith was killed and his body mutilated simply because he bore the name John Knox, while a servant of John Craig was imprisoned when he nervously blurted out that his master was John Knox. In exile Knox consoled himself by teaching St Andrews' students in the fierce faith he espoused and indoctrinating them against the Marians and all their works. This faith permitted him the satisfaction of watching a morality play put on by one of the regents of St Leonard's College depicting the siege and capture of Edinburgh Castle, and Grange being hanged in effigy. Likewise the old prophet of St Giles must have praised God and smiled knowingly when he heard news that two of the soldiers who had despoiled the steeple with their fortifications and even baptised one of the noisy double falcons placed there with the name Knox, were killed when it burst from over-firing. 'This they get from mocking God's servants', quipped the sanctimonious Bannatyne.[12]

The English were again worried that the Regent and his supporters, left to their own devices, could not settle the matter. Drury was sent back to Scotland 'to travail to obtain a surcease of arms on both sides so that it may be beneficial to the King's party.' Here we see the thrust of Elizabeth's policy: peace, but on terms favourable to the Jacobean side. The imminence of English intervention concentrated minds, and the diplomatic war recommenced. 'The fire of unkindness' between Lennox and Morton had been well and truly kindled over the months and it was well-known that the latter served 'impatiently' under the Regent. Disunity among their enemies and the enervating paralysis it could engender was encouraged by the Marians whenever they could.[13] As part of this ploy, Grange wrote to Morton criticising Lennox for delaying a settlement until his parliament met, and for intending to bring troops to Edinburgh. If Lennox and his nobles wanted to come to Edinburgh to negotiate a peace treaty in accordance with Elizabeth's urging, the town would be thrown open to them and they could come and go unscathed. But if they came to subdue the town to their will they would gain no admittance other than that they could purchase by force. Morton assured Grange that he would pass on the message to the council and that he too wanted the realm to stay in quietness, but pointedly adding 'who has given occasion of the disturbance thereof, yourself can testify, who was with me at the beginning.'[14]

Morton, the 'strongest man in Scotland' as the English perceived, was not to be seduced by his antipathy for Lennox, nor deflected from his primary goal, the retaking of the capital. Two days after this exchange, on Wednesday 9 May, Morton and the Regent concentrated their forces around Edinburgh. Morton barracked his most reliable professional troops at Dalkeith, at once a body guard and a mobile troop to patrol the countryside and prevent the Castilians from pillaging it. He could now reply to Grange's overtures in full having sounded out the council. He castigated the Keeper of the Castle, 'a private man' who, by virtue of the Castle bestowed upon him in trust for the King, presumed 'to dictate to the Regent, nobility and estates how they shall act and what deliberate upon in Parliament!' He would be judged the author of all the misfortunes that might follow and 'if any suffer as a result of your unreasonable stance their blood shall be required at your hands.' It was, of course, signed 'your good friend, Morton.'[15]

Grange was not a bit intimidated. When on the Friday the Regent came to Leith with 5,000 horse his request to enter Edinburgh was turned down by the council. Edinburgh locked its gates and manned its defences. Some prominent Marian supporters, such as James Mossman, the jeweller, and his brother-in-law James Cockie, took refuge in the Castle, the former abandoning his lovely home at the Netherbow, now known as John Knox House. Grange declared a 9 p.m. curfew and again ordered all the remaining sympathisers of the Regent to leave within the hour. A number of overt supporters of the King's party were forcibly evicted from the capital while others, more neutral, realising that neutrality was not an option, chose to remove to Leith, to ensure that there could be no misunderstanding that by remaining in Edinburgh they were offering practical succour to the Queen. The Queen's lords were wary of anarchy and concerned to avoid conjuring up the chilling memories of the reoccupation of the town by the French troops of Mary of Guise in 1559.[16]

On the evening of Sunday 13 May, the Regent's men positioned three pieces of ordnance on the Dow Crag or Pigeon's Rock, a prominence on the southern slope of the Cragingate overlooking Trinity College in Leith Wynd. From this vantage point their battery could defend the Canongate and attack the north-east quarter of the Burgh as far as St Giles. There were several fatalities as a result, including Captain Gibson who was in charge of the steeple, and one soldier called Kirkcaldy who had been accustomed to dance round the cock on the steeple baring his buttocks at the enemy. To kill a lewd Kirkcaldy boded well for the future. A strong contingent under Crawford of Jordanhill occupied two houses at the head of Leith Wynd, and from their safe haven shot at the troops on the two turrets above the Netherbow Port and on civilians beneath. This was proving a weak point, and all available workmen were commanded to come with their spades and mattocks to barricade the gate, infilling it with muck, stones and timber. It was a noble company of labourers including Huntly, Home, Claud and his brothers, John and Gavin, that toiled through the night and completed their job before dawn. Bannatyne disdainfully commented that 'the laird of Grange is become a great man now, when sic men are pioneers to him.'[17]

The Castilians erected four earth-filled gun emplacements by the Netherbow Port where they could cannonade the gate if need be, and brought the great bombard, Mons Meg, down to Blackfriars Yard where it proceeded to do considerable damage to houses at the head of the Canongate until it was forced by the fading light to retire to the security of the Castle. The following day it was again brought down, this time at the cost of two or three men losing their lives pulling it. When a number of its guard were killed by one of its cannon balls igniting the gabrons, and the gunners themselves came under heavy fire from a house in the Pleasance the bombard was removed for good after it had discharged no more than two dozen shot.[18]

The Regent, however, lacked sufficient cannon of his own to storm the town and made no attempt to undermine it. Nor could he take it by force of numbers. The whole contingent in Edinburgh was estimated at 6,000-7,000, compared with the 5,000-6,000 men the Regent could muster. To his chagrin

23 Mons Meg, the great bombard.

he neither had power enough to hold his parliament in the traditional venue of the Tolbooth nor to evict the Marians who held their own parliament there, a rival assembly dignified if not by legitimacy at least by the semblance of it: the crown, sword and sceptre which Grange brought out from his safe-keeping in the Castle. Grange refused to surrender the regalia for the Regent's parliament. It was held nonetheless since it was judged 'no more a sin to hold a parliament without these ceremonies than a bishop needeth to make scruple to preach without his rotchet, mitre and ring.'[19] The Regent's parliament was relegated to William Cocker's house, near St John's Cross in the Canongate. Here, within the liberties of the city, which lawyers alone could maintain was as good as if it had been within the walls, while the cannon of the Castle opened upon them, the King's party assembled for what became known as the 'creeping parliament' from the number of times that its members had to take to their hands and knees to avoid salvos from the Castle. In this posture they uttered impotent anathemas against Lethington, his brother and others of their opponents. Each night shots from the Castle would pursue the Regent on his way to Leith. The fatalities included the master gunner, a boy, an Englishman and two women. Others were hurt. Psychologically the damage was worse, and after five days of this endurance test they could take no more. The Regent adjourned the sitting until August and he and Morton withdrew to Leith with a large part of their forces and all their artillery. The last hours of the siege were played out in high farce when an attempt to ambush the Regent's rearguard in the Canongate resulted in only one fatality – a poor camp-follower too slow to escape when he was caught with his hose down while relieving himself in a trench.[20]

On Sunday 20 May 1571 the first siege of Edinburgh was formally raised. Early in the morning the Regent and 1,500 men decamped for Stirling, leaving Morton and his men to keep watch on the capital. His first task was to ensure the safe passage of the Regent on his way to Linlithgow. He proceeded out of Leith with a troop of 500 horsemen and, skirting Edinburgh to the north under desultory fire from the Castle, he positioned himself on the ridge of a hill keeping watch until Lennox was safe. While this was going on, the Edinburgh garrison issued out and followed them as far as Corstorphine where Morton and his escort turned south-east. The Castilians marched half a mile to intercept him at the Boroughmuir. There they offered battle but Morton uncharacteristically declined and struck off in a different direction for Dalkeith. It was rumoured that the 'cause of this hasty passage was because his soldiers wanted both powder and bullets.'[21] It was either that or because he could not lure the Castilians out of range of the Castle's guns.

Frustrated of their game, the Castilian forces returned to town to see what pickings could be found. Curious soldiers, rooting round Cuthbert Ferguson's house in the Canongate, so recently vacated by the Regent, discovered to their delight three or four tuns of wine, as well as the more useful but less pleasing packs of wool and skins brought from Leith to help protect the house from cannon fire.[22] Grange's troops even entered Leith unopposed and seized provisions, including another stock of wine and brewing implements. What they could not carry off they destroyed.

Grange and his forces had the Burgh to themselves for the first time. Further security – and to some vindictive – measures were rapidly implemented. These included the systematic demolition of the houses in Leith Wynd and St Mary's Wynd at the head of the Canongate to prevent the Regent's men from again using their roofs as platforms from which to fire down on those inside the city walls. This began on 9 June under Captain James Cullen and was done in a peremptory manner, their owners being ordered into the streets with little time to salvage their belongings before the buildings were reduced to piles of dust and rubble. The Burgh houses on the west side of St Mary's Wynd were rendered more defensible by having all their windows and doors blocked up and their forestairs removed.[23] There was no resistance.

Elizabeth, dismayed by this turn of events, again intervened, sending Drury to remonstrate with Grange about his hostile acts in amassing great numbers

24 The Netherbow Port, *c*.1764. John Knox House is on the right. The gate was rebuilt after the civil war but occupied the same site as the old Port.

of soldiers, fortifying the town and spreading slanders that the Regent was a puppet of England.[24] At the same time Drury was to assess what help the Regent needed to take the Castle and was authorised to bestow 200 harquebusiers to safeguard the King in Stirling. Grange and Lethington both knew that any threat of intervention by England had to be taken seriously and defused if at all possible. England could be decisive against them. They launched a dual charm offensive. Lethington sent the English Queen an impassioned letter – or apologia – protesting that he was the victim of evil calumnies. On Moray's assassination he had tried to bring about reconciliation, but failed. He had tried to retire, but Elizabeth herself wanted him to treat with Argyll and Huntly. He had been deposed from his office and, during the abstinence, his enemies had seized his house and goods. He refused to stand by and let five or six minor Earls tread their betters underfoot. In the King's name they were destroying his kingdom and he would inherit 'a confused chaos and a country divided into 200 or 300 Kingdoms whereof everyone will be a King in his own bounds – or in ten miles compass!' Lethington mocked at the suggestion that he had seduced Grange, 'a man not led by other men's persuasions,' promised not to bring foreign troops into Scotland and offered to submit all outstanding issues to Elizabeth's arbitration.[25] On the same day, Grange in turn wrote protesting that he was a victim of misreports. He had not wanted to continue the civil war, but merely resisted the aggression of the Lennox party. He and his colleagues had not wanted to seek help abroad, but with their lands despoiled, and their revenues withheld, they were reduced to asking France for munitions. Yet he too was ready to promise that no foreign troops would be brought into Scotland, and he too was ready to negotiate under her mediation.[26]

Elizabeth was impressed by the reasonable tone of these missives. This was in marked contrast to the attitude of the Regent who was clearly pursuing a personal vendetta under the mask of constitutionality. His precarious parliament had become little more than an instrument of private revenge, producing nothing other than wholesale forfeitures of the Marians' lands. Elizabeth ordered him to hold such measures in abeyance since they were jeopardising her genuine desire for a peaceful settlement. No offer of English help was proffered. She was concerned that if Lennox took her support for granted he would not want to settle for the cheaper option, but would make 'large demands,' of her, demands she was not eager to meet.[27] She was right. Lennox begged Elizabeth for men, money and munitions. In the bidding war for 100 Danish mercenaries recently arrived in Scotland, he needed English gold to counter the French gold being proffered by the Castilians. To take the town and Castle he needed cannons, culverins and batteries with powder, bullets and pioneers.[28] This was just the sort of involvement Elizabeth deplored. She ordered Drury to get the two sides to negotiate and to lay down their arms, as Grange and Lethington had already offered to do.

The laying down of arms, however, would present a problem. Neither side could forebear trying to get the upper-hand militarily, whatever the diplomatic developments. Violent encounters, characterised by ever-increasing brutality, punctuated the days for the best part of the next two years, causing more havoc and distress than in the last days of Mary of Guise, or even, some said, during the 'Rough Wooing.'[29]

25 A demi-culverin, c.1570 – not in its original mountings.

6

THE DOUGLAS WARS BEGIN
June to August 1571

The remanent they drove to Leith like sheep stobbing and dunting them
with spears where they were all hangit without furder process: and this
form of dealing was callit the Douglas Wars.[1]

The first really serious skirmish of what contemporaries came to call the
'Douglas Wars' took place on a rain-drenched Saturday 2 June at Edmonston
Edge, near Craigmillar Castle. Morton in his capacity of enforcing the
blockade was proving the most formidable foe to the Castilians. His castle at
Dalkeith was the major base for intercepting supplies heading for the Castle,
and his men put up the toughest resistance. The Castilians received intelligence
that he had dispatched part of his force as an escort for the Regent and had
only 200 men left. Hoping to surprise him with his depleted force and burn
his village, a raiding party of 220 foot, 100 horse and two falcons (portable field
pieces) under the command of Captain Melville set off for Dalkeith. They
marched through the night and lashing rain, and were cold and very wet by
the time they got to Lugton Brae, within a half-mile of their goal. There the
bedraggled company was spotted by a local woman who ran back to Dalkeith
to raise the alarm.

With amazing rapidity Morton drew up in line of battle in the open fields.
The Edinburgh contingent, faced with such unexpected resistance, and
discovering that their sodden guns were rendered virtually useless, retired in
good order towards the city. Morton's men pursued them for three miles until
the Castilians descended the long brae of Edmonston, dragged their cannon
through a burn, and gained the summit of Craigmillar Hill. Here they rallied
and wheeled round their falcons to cannonade Morton's men as they marched
down the opposite slope. In the urgency of the moment, Melville began

26 The siege of Leith, 1560. The plan gives a good idea of the dimensions of the two towns and of the countryside in between. Not much would have changed in the layout between 1560 and a decade later, although the French fortifications around Leith were dismantled in 1561.

disbursing powder from a barrel strapped to the back of a sumpter. As the cannoneers crowded round a spark from one of their matches caused the powder to explode, killing two men outright and injuring many others including Melville who was blown into the air and mortally wounded. Once more the Castilians turned and fled, encumbered now by their wounded. Morton's mounted harquebusiers caught up with them at a little hamlet called Lady-brig-end on the other side of Craigmillar Hill and charged. Many were speared and shot on both sides and a running fight was maintained for a mile between Craigmillar and the gibbet near the old farm of St Giles' Grange. Morton called off the pursuit at this point, since his men were exhausted and the Castle guns were beginning to play on them. Four days later, when Melville died of his wounds, his nephew drew up his men inside the blockhouse of the Castle and encouraged them to remain loyal and true in the face of the loss of such a leader.[2] As a demonstration of his confidence or chivalry, Grange was prepared to exchange ten of Morton's men taken in the skirmish for a badly injured youth who was being held for execution.[3]

To undermine Grange's high standing, his enemies resorted to vilification. He was made the butt of every slander and calumny spread by word of mouth and surreptitious handbill. An honourable man who set much store by his good name, he exploded in rage at those who were 'lying in their throats' by calling him a traitor, a murderer and an accomplice in the murder of Moray 'for whom I hazzarded all I had in the world.' If he knew who the authors were – of whatever estate, degree or quality – he 'would answer them more particularly.' Things got so heated that when one of his most virulent detractors, Alexander Stewart, the son of the Laird of Garleis, challenged him to single combat he rashly agreed. His confrères, however, would not let him risk his neck and their cause in this quixotic act of personal revenge, and no more came of it.[4]

On 12 June Drury arrived back in Edinburgh with instructions to broker a peace. He was welcomed by a parliament held in the Tolbooth, with Chatelherault, Huntly, Home, Herries and a few others attending. The Duke bore the crown, Huntly the sceptre, Home the sword. It was a pretty meagre showing, hardly meriting the title 'parliament,' but again the appurtenances of legitimacy Grange had refused the King's parliament he bestowed on the Queen's. An Act was immediately passed, annulling Mary's abdication as made under duress and declaring the King's coronation null and void. When Drury expressed the mild rebuke that it was a little precipitate to hold this parliament before receiving word from Elizabeth whom they had sought to be mediatrix, Grange glibly reassured him that the Queen would not object to their actions.[5]

The citizens of Edinburgh were enjoined to acknowledge Queen Mary as sovereign and no other, and the Kirk ministers, Galloway and Craig, were commanded to pray for the Queen during services. When the latter refused he was banned from preaching.[6] Craig had been actively neutral for some time, saying plainly and publicly from his pulpit that he considered both sides to be at fault, and that any victory would be pyrrhic in as much as the country would be ruined. The sentiments he preached sprang from his 'peaceful temper in wishing the breach to be made up.'[7] Such eirenicism had not been known in St Giles for many a long year, and such a stance was not designed to win friends. By contrast the Sunday homily of his colleague and Huntly's uncle, Alexander Gordon, Bishop of Galloway, was on 'charity,' and his theme was that Mary's moral failings did not disqualify her as a monarch. 'Sanct David was a sinner, and so is she; Sanct David was an adulterer and so is she; Sanct David committed murder in slaying Uriah for his wife, and so did she; but what is this to the matter? The more wicked she be her subjects should pray for her to bring her to the spirit of repentance... No inferior subject had power to deprive or depose their lawful magistrate.' While hardly a ringing endorsement of the Queen as a person, these sentiments accurately echoed the views of many of her supporters, including Grange and Lethington.[8]

On Saturday 16 June the Castilians, who had heard that Morton was ill and were as anxious to make amends for their failure two weeks before as to demonstrate their superiority in front of the English agent, headed in battle order for Leith. Huntly, Gavin Hamilton and John Maitland were in charge of the foot, Buccleugh and Fernihurst of the horse. In addition they brought along their two falcons to show their worth in dry conditions. They approached as far as the Gallowlee near Leith and the cavalry took up position between the quarries of Craggingate and Hawkhill – a rocky, wooded knoll beside Lochend Loch – with the infantry behind them on the slopes of Abbeyhill. Morton, enraged at their temerity, and forgetting his own infirmity, got out of his bed, marched his men out of the town and took up battle order on Hawkhill itself less than half a mile from the enemy cavalry. He had three companies of mercenary foot, a squadron of cavalry and a bodyguard of pikemen, a sizeable professional force supplemented by a group of armed exiles. Drury who had accompanied Morton galloped between the armies and made them promise not to fight that day. Neither was willing to retire first, so Drury proposed to stand in the middle, and give a signal for both to retire at once. What happened thereafter is open to debate. Either the Castilians refused to comply and brought up their artillery, or, much more likely, Morton launched a surprise attack when his opponents were retiring. Whatever the case, Morton's men soon prevailed over their more numerous enemies by a precipitate cavalry charge which threw back the Marian horse upon their own footmen causing chaos. Morton's infantry advanced towards the disordered enemy and delivered a salvo, but before hand-to-hand fighting was joined, Huntly and his men turned tail and fled through the old village of Abbeyhill, past Mary of Guise's house of Croft-an-Righ. Many were slaughtered among the thick hedges, grey walls and summer orchards of those old suburbs. The survivors ran through the low-browed arch of the Watergate beside the Abbey, and rushed into the Canongate. Only those in the Abbey churchyard made a show of resistance but were soon forced to flee down the narrow street towards the Netherbow Port with the rest. Some were cut down by the riders, some trampled under foot by the horses, some crushed to death in the throng, and the rest ran away so fast and in such disorder that they forgot to shut the gates at the Netherbow. Had their pursuers not stopped to pillage they might easily have taken the city. Nonetheless it was a stunning victory at little cost. Gavin Hamilton and thirty other Castilians died in this encounter, and many valuable horses were lost. The two ill-fated pieces of ordnance and around 150 shamefaced prisoners were taken to Leith, the chief of whom was Lord Home, who had been slightly injured by falling from his horse. As a valuable commodity he was freed in a prisoner exchange a month later. Another prominent prize was the notorious Captain Cullen, the distinguished but detested veteran of the army of Mary of Guise, who suffered the indignity of being found hidden in a pantry, pulled out by his heels and dragged to Leith, with the mob baying for his blood. Back in the Burgh, treason was suspected by many, and Drury blamed by all. The skirmish became known to both sides as 'Drury's Peace' and to the Castilians as 'Black Saturday.'[9]

As a result of this near debacle, the Marian grip on Edinburgh grew tighter and attempts to root out dissent gathered apace. Up until this point the Burgh administration had continued as before. McGill the Provost and all four baillies were still in post, clinging on in the hope that the Marians would withdraw. This could not continue. A loyal citizenry was vital to the security of the Castilians. On 20 June Grange deposed the Provost and magistrates, and expelled the town council, installing his henchmen as baillies and his own son-in-law, Thomas Kerr of Fernihurst as Provost.

27 Sir Thomas Kerr of Fernihurst.

To safeguard the revenue the custumar, Robert Watson, a consistent Protestant activist throughout the 1560s, was replaced by Cuthbert Ramsay, one of the new baillies, and to ensure a compliant pulpit a new Kirk Session was appointed. On 23 June some 200 members of the deposed Burgh establishment removed themselves to Leith and stayed there, despite a proclamation threatening forfeiture of their goods if they did not return. Provocatively, there they formed and financed an armed militia called the 'Edinburgh Band,' made Adam Fullerton, the expelled dean of guild, their captain, and enrolled themselves in the Regent's service 'to restore the whole polity within that town.' A fortnight later the Queen's men paraded the new baillies through the Burgh and mustered 600 men in Greyfriar's yard. Led by two ensigns carrying Marian banners, they then marched towards Leith in contemptuous mockery of the exiles and their militia. The exiles responded with a muster of half the size and, when they marched out of Leith, Grange was ready for them and sent them scurrying with a few shots from his cannon. In retaliation, the captive Captain Cullen was tried and convicted of treason that very same day, and beheaded a few days later on Leith links, 'greatly to the contentation of the people' – especially the women. Hostilities between the rival groups were rapidly escalating into the increasingly bitter war of attrition which was to characterise the succeeding fifteen months.[10]

The Regent was at a tactical disadvantage. He had both to spread his limited manpower over the country and yet maintain pressure on Edinburgh by cutting it off from its supplies of food and fuel. For all his efforts, Morton on his own with his roving patrols had been unable to prevent reinforcements coming to the Castle. To cut off the town, Lennox had to invest it. To the north lay his main base at Leith whose fortifications he repaired, to the east was Morton in Dalkeith, and by the end of June a 6-foot deep trench had been dug around the east and south-east of Edinburgh, the most difficult area to police. The Regent garrisoned strategic points – Corstorphine, Craigmillar, Edmonston and elsewhere – to seize provisions heading for the town by land, and commissioned a two-gun pinnace to intercept any shipping bringing aid to the rebels – with Dumbarton denied them, all attempts would have to be on the east coast.[11] This later precaution was early rewarded with two considerable prizes. The first was the seizure on 30 June of John Chisholm, Master of the Ordnance of Scotland no less, when he landed at Burntisland with 7,400 French francs, several barrels of gun powder and ammunition, 1,000 hagbuts and 200 pikes, all meant for the Castle. Yet even this success was tarnished by the Regent purloining some of the money for himself and by the

Castilians managing to retrieve or destroy most of their munitions in a raid a few days later. The second was the capture in the Firth of Forth of Verac, returning from France with all his diplomatic correspondence. He was safely banished out of harm's way to St Andrews.[12] Or so they thought. The net round Edinburgh had large holes. Slow moving supplies could be intercepted but flying columns from the Castle were far harder to frustrate. In a daring overnight ride, David Spens of Wormiston, an accomplished young captain of horse, and five others reached St Andrews and conducted Verac back to Edinburgh, seizing Lord Lindsay's best horses at Anstruther in the process. The same day other horsemen raided his house of the Byers near Haddington in Lothian, and brought back 100 head of cattle to the Castle. Again the Regent's painstaking measures had been made a mockery of. Other ploys must be tried.[13]

The Regent's substantial garrison at Holyrood remained the nearest threat to the Castilians and attempts to eradicate it were inevitable. During the few hours of darkness on Friday 13 July Castilian troops emerged from the Netherbow to launch a surprise attack on those in the Abbey but their approach was noticed and they were soon sent packing by resolute fire from Captain Mitchell's well-entrenched veterans. The Marians then placed heavy ordnance in Blackfriar's yard to fire on Holyrood, but to little effect.[14] The

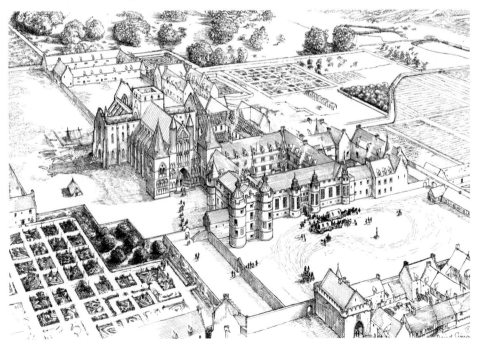

28 Reconstruction of Holyrood Palace, c.1560.

29 James VI at the time of the Stirling parliament. This precocious six-year-old
already has a regal bearing and his love of hunting is evident by the bird of prey he
is holding.

Castilians were justified in their concern about enclaves of enemy troops too
near their citadel. One night a boy was sent to the Netherbow Port purporting
to bring a letter from Fernihurst. They opened the gate but he ran off calling
them traitors. When they gave pursuit they were attacked by a detachment
from the Abbey and forced back in, closing the gate just in time.[15] Another
stratagem to take the town on the morning of 22 August was foiled but only

fortuitously. Early in the morning a dozen horses laden with meal were to be brought in at the Netherbow by soldiers in disguise. After they had entered they were to pull out their concealed weapons, overcome the guards and secure the gate. Other soldiers who had been hiding in nearby closes, houses and barns, along with two companies of foot who were standing ready in the Abbey, would complete the conquest. However, an early bird from the town, one Tom Barrie, came out of the Netherbow to go to his own house in the Canongate. Spying armed men crammed into every lane, he rushed back shouting 'Treason!' The gates were immediately shut. The poor man, however, was left outside and the Regent ordered him to have his hand struck off for 'counterfeiting his hand.'[16] The Netherbow was an obviously vulnerable spot. Almost immediately work began building a new gate inside the old, a gate that was constructed of the finest ashlar to give it greater strength, and which had two gun-holes behind which were positioned heavy cannon.[17]

Despite the fall of Dumbarton, further progress eluded the Regent. The rival groups were skirmishing inconclusively, not getting in a death grip. He decided to rally the troops for a further concerted effort to deal with the Castilian problem once and for all, and summoned his supporters to attend a parliament to be held in the royal presence at Stirling on 28 August. A new crown, sceptre and sword were commissioned for the occasion because the old ones were still in Edinburgh. At the appointed time and place the party of the King gathered in all their strength, a strength enhanced by the presence of Argyll.

The Earl had recently become the first person of stature to defect from the Queen's party, although he was soon to be followed by Cassilis, Boyd and Eglinton. His move had not come out of the blue. He had wavered before and had been the first to submit to Moray two years earlier. In May it had been rumoured that he had become disenchanted with the obduracy of the Castilians in the face of reasonable proposals from the Regent. Disenchantment had soon led to desertion. He was made much of by his new friends and soon benefited by his betrayal.

The assembly – dubbed the 'Black Parliament' by Grange – forfeited their enemies as their enemies had forfeited them, and promised each other the spoil. More importantly they resolved to go to Edinburgh with all their forces and win the town.[18] Before they could take action, however, an ominous note crept in. The young King, who graced their proceedings with his presence, with the sharp wandering eye of a bored child, noticed a small aperture in the roof. He memorably pronounced that there was a hole in his parliament. Some deemed this quip inauspicious for the unpopular Regent. So it proved to be. A week later he was dead, with a hole in his back.[19]

7

THE STIRLING RAID
3 and 4 September 1571

'A pleasant and profitable time for murderers, thieves, and such as live
only by the spoils of true men.'
Lord Hunsdon[1]

Border men whose minds are only given to reif and spuilyie.[2]

The Castilians struck first. Grange devised a plan which, had it been as successful as it was audacious, would have ended the conflict virtually bloodlessly and in total victory for the Marians. He proposed a night ride on Stirling to capture all the leaders of the King's faction. Despite the fact that they had some 2,000 retainers with them, Grange thought a small raiding party could surprise them while they were asleep, unsuspecting and defenceless. Such a *coup de main* would repay the Dumbarton debacle and more. Fatally, the mastermind of the plot was told he must not go on so risky a venture. Instead the expedition was cursed with five leaders: Huntly, Kerr of Fernihurst, Claud Hamilton, Scott of Buccleuch and Spens of Wormiston. Between them they commanded a striking force of sixty mounted hagbutters and 340 Border Horse, lightly armoured, steel-bonneted, deadly.[3]

In the early evening of 3 September the raiding party rode out of the Cowgate Port having sent a forward party of light horse to the Queen's Ferry and other points on the road to Stirling to detain all travellers and prevent information being carried ahead of them. They made a feint towards Peebles and news soon got back to Leith that they were heading to attack Jedburgh.[4] Under cover of dark, they wheeled off in the direction of Stirling. When they reached within a mile of their goal they dismounted, tethered their horses and stealthily approached the town on foot. Huntly had recruited George Bell as their guide. Although he was an ensign bearer to a company in Edinburgh, he

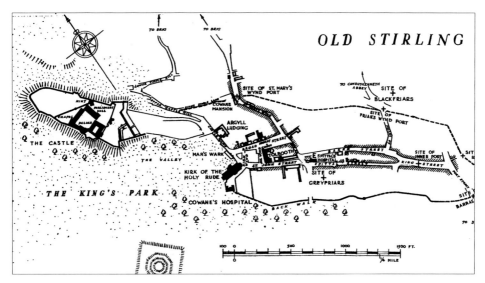

30 Map of old Stirling showing the Castle, Mar's Wark, and the Barras Yett.

was a Stirling man born and bred who knew every nook and cranny, every back street and alley, in the town. He also knew the lodgings of every nobleman attending the parliament and the paucity of the watch.

Like Edinburgh, the old town of Stirling clung to the spine of a ridge descending eastwards from the castle. The first houses were about a bowshot from the outer fortifications and from them stretched the High Street [Broad Street] with the Tolbooth on its southern side and the parish church on its south-west corner. Various wynds ran off on either side. The whole was enclosed by a strong wall on its most vulnerable southern and eastern flanks, and by a lesser system of dykes and walls to the north. Several gates, the most elaborate of which was the great Barras Port or Yett on the south-east corner of the town allowed official access, but its defences were porous when not well watched. In the grey of the morning after the night watchman had gone to bed and before the inhabitants were stirring the raiders silently entered the town by a narrow passage. Once they had reached the market cross they cried 'God and the Queen!' and 'A Hamilton! Remember the Bishop of St Andrews! All is ours!' They occupied every street without difficulty, broke open the nobles' houses, and captured the Regent, Glencairn, Argyll, Cassilis, Eglington, Montrose and Buchan along with the Lords Semple, Cathcart and Ochiltree. Lennox caved in as soon as he was told that there was powder in the vaults, as in the Kirk o' Field! Stout resistance came from Morton alone who galvanised his men and barricaded his house which stood at the foot of the

79

31 Prospect of Stirling from the east. The castle is on the right of the town.

High Street. From its grates his men fired on their assailants, Morton in the thick of it. He was finally forced to surrender when his house was fired around him and some of his men were killed, but he had won time. By 7 a.m. the Castilians were masters of the town. Only Mar and Angus were safe in the castle. The captives were placed under house arrest, and were to be conducted down the High Street to the Barras Yett where the raiding party intended to re-mount their horses and ride to Edinburgh with their rich prize. Speed was of the essence, speed and cohesion, before the superior forces lodged in the castle and town could be galvanised against them. But the wild Borderers, rather than keeping together to guard their invaluable prize as they were hurried out of the town, dispersed in search of more ephemeral booty.

The Hamiltons too played their part in compromising the endeavour. When Lord Claud and his men came towards the captive Morton, Buccleugh, who was not only an honourable man, but the captive Earl's kin by marriage, understandably feared that they would kill his prisoner. He would not wait for

Lennox and the other captives to be assembled and taken off together, but rushed Morton down the street towards the Barras Yett, leaving Huntly and Lord Claud with a seriously depleted force. Meanwhile Mar emerged from the castle with forty men and two small cannon but was unable to enter the narrow wynds since all were well guarded. The raiders, however, had overlooked one building, Mar's Wark, the Regent's own half-built town house. It was strategically placed with the castle to its rear, and the wide expanse of the High Street exposed before it. Mar sent sixteen of his men to take up position in it. They entered by the back gate, and climbed to the windows on the top floor, directly overlooking the enemy. From there they shot into the thickest of them with deadly effect. Their fire drove Huntly and his prisoners from the market place. When Captain Crawford sallied out of the castle Huntly and his men were driven by weight of numbers further down the slope of the street towards St Ninian's Church and the Barras Yett.[5] Buccleugh was taken at the Port, and Morton, Eglington and Glencairn were rescued. They snatched up such weapons as they could from the dead around them and soon put their enemies to rout. Glencairn himself turned tables on his captor, John Hamilton of Cilbouie and took him prisoner. The Castilians made it back to their horses and rode off, leaving nine men dead and sixteen captured. The

32 Mar's Wark as a ruin. Before its completion in 1572 the future Regent's elaborate town house would have looked much like this, less the foliage.

King's side lost seventeen slain, including Alexander Stewart, younger of Garleis who was killed in the melee at the Port. Thirty-seven were seriously wounded. The rebels took away with them 320 horses and a lot of valuable plunder, but not the invaluable hostages their whole enterprise had been designed to capture.

The guerilla action which could have ended the war decisively in favour or the Marians had little to show, and the one major fatality on the other side had been better left alive. This was the Regent Lennox who was shot in the back while being escorted down a side street when his captors realised they would not be able to get him away.[6] He had been made prisoner by Spens of Wormiston. Spens, who had been told by Grange to save Lennox from the vengeance of the Hamiltons, had nobly interposed his own body to protect his prisoner from the assassin and was badly wounded as a result. He was put out of his misery by the Regent's soldiers who hacked him to pieces, despite the dying Lennox imploring mercy for his saviour. This scene occurred near the Barras Yett, and a cairn of stones marking the spot survived there until 1758.[7] Mortally wounded, the Regent managed to ride into the castle and summon the chief noblemen to his deathbed. Commending the King to their care and his dependants to their charity, he made a good death later that evening. He was buried in the royal chapel at Stirling Castle.

A swift vengeance overtook his assassin, whoever he was. Both George Bell and James Calder were taken, both were racked, and both claimed to be that man, the rack working its usual persuasion in gaining confessions. Their instructions from Grange had been to capture the Regent, not to kill him. The Regent's death, confessed Calder, 'with my hand laid on the pen because I cannot write,' had been ordered by Claud Hamilton and Huntly in revenge for the killing of the Archbishop of St Andrews. Morton too should have been slain and Ruthven and James MacGill 'should have tasted of the same cup'. Tortured out of him or no, these revelations had the aura of truth, and did 'not a little kindle the fire of hate towards them.' Both men were then dispatched: Bell being hanged; Calder 'after the manner of France,' his arms and legs being broken on the wheel while he yet lived.[8]

In reality, the death of Lennox was a disaster for the Castilian cause, ridding their enemies of an unpopular Regent, making him a martyr, and bringing in a better replacement under whom they could all unite. Grange realised this. 'We regret most the slaughter of Lennox, because thereby the adverse faction have obtained what they have long sought by many means – that was to be rid of him.'[9] He – and others – even speculated that the Regent might have been killed by his own side deliberately or by accident.[10] Although Grange could

33 The Regent Mar 'who loved peace and could not have it'.

boast of his men's achievement of entering and holding Stirling in the face of the King's lords and all their retinues, he knew that for lack of his presence they had lost a magnificent chance to rid Scotland of a large swathe of the King's party. By the indiscipline of the Borderers and the costly kindness of Buccleugh towards Morton 'the whole fruit of the journey was lost.' He ruefully concluded that 'our men hes honour and advantage over meikle, but we esteem it nothing in respect that all Earls and lords of the adverse faction were not brought to Edinburgh.'[11]

The botched Stirling coup was the turning point. Had it succeeded, resistance would have collapsed and the Marians would have won. Not only did it fail but it removed from the scene the one man the Marians should have kept alive, the Regent whose unpopularity had helped sustain them. Only after the election of Lennox's successor did the full-scale siege of Edinburgh begin in earnest. But who would succeed? Morton was England's choice and England's man but he was abrasive and divisive and the Scottish lords preferred the more emollient Mar, their gratitude to him for rescuing them from Grange's troopers contributing to his successful elevation. He was a man whom even Morton conceded to be 'both godly, honest and of upright nature.' Morton could afford to be generous. He knew he would become the *de facto* ruler of Scotland during Mar's regency, and thereafter *de iure* as well.

8

MONEY IS THE MAN
September to December 1571

Money is the Man in Scotland.

William Drury[1]

The dire straits of the Castilians shortly after the botched Stirling raid replicated and surpassed their desperate state after the fall of Dumbarton. With the defection of Argyll, the wavering of other leading Marians, and worry obvious on the face of even the most resolute, confidence among the canny merchant class was undermined and local fiscal support began to haemorrhage. Few would deal with the Castilians, all demanded payment on account and none would give credit.[2] Meanwhile things would only get worse, since intelligence suggested that the new Regent was going to muster all his forces at Leith to invest Edinburgh and starve it into submission.

Great preparations were made to defend the town from the expected onslaught. Some were the product of foresight. Provisions had been stockpiled to last the winter, and over the previous twelve months the Castilians had gathered as much turf and earth as they could, vital for muffling the effect of cannon fire. Several citizens whose sympathies were doubted were taken into protective custody in the Castle and held under threat of execution. The closes on the east side of the Burgh, still the most vulnerable part of the defences, were blocked up to the dismay of their owners. A trench was constructed within the wall, and all the lanes that led into the High Street were cut. Heavy ordnance were placed at strategic points in the town, including another cannon in Blackfriars' yard to shoot into the Canongate. The English assessment was that the town was so well fortified that if it could be captured it would only be with great slaughter, and that the Castle was much stronger than heretofore, with all the deficiencies in its defence made good.[3]

34 Edinburgh, prospect from North, by John Slezer.

Yet when the second siege began on Tuesday 16 October, scarcely ten per-
cent of the inhabitants remained in Edinburgh – even Grange's own daughter
fled – so widespread was the expectation of Mar's victory. Those who
remained worked tirelessly in defence of their town, manning the walls,
keeping watch under fire.[4] Their fears were unjustified and the siege petered
out after a week since the resources available to the Regent were totally
insufficient for the task of a major siege. Money as always was short, and to pay
his troops, Mar was reduced to the unpopular expedient of taxing merchants
coming into Dalkeith. The most serious deficiency was in siege ordnance and
its appurtenances. Without the loan of heavy artillery from England, the
Regent had had to order that battering pieces be stripped from the other major
fortresses of Dumbarton, Stirling and Dunbar, and brought by sea to Leith. By
such exigencies he had managed to muster merely seven pieces of ordnance –
a demi cannon, a culverin, two demi-culverins, a brass saker and two
dismounted iron demi-culverins – and even these outnumbered the trained
gunners. Twelve barrels of powder at one point constituted the arsenal.
Elementary entrenching materials such as picks and shovels were in short
supply, and the only planks they had were of deal, not strong enough to bear
the cannon.[5]

Mar tried to reduce Grange by bombarding the city from John Adamson's
house on the east side of the Pleasance. From this vantage point in the
Canongate the gun fired repeatedly at Adam Fullarton's house and the gun
platform which Grange had erected there, but with little effect. The besiegers
turned their attention to two sections of the Flodden Wall. On 18 October,

after a labourious pounding and the expenditure of 180 cannon balls, they breached the southern wall of the city to reveal strongly manned inner defences and cannon still in place trained on the breach. These factors coupled with lack of ammunition prevented an assault. The desultory artillery bombardment continued for another three days, inflicting most damage not to military installations but to the houses and shops of the townspeople. Both the Thief Row and the Potter Row went up in flames. Misfortune added to frustration and began to tell on the Regent. Of the two pieces of small ordnance Mar placed upon Salisbury Hill one blew up and Cuthbert Ramsay, the King's trench master was killed, while Grange's cannoneers fired their light guns from the spires of St Giles and Kirk o' Field so expertly that one of their balls went through the pavilion of the Regent, killing twelve of his attendants. Battered, the King's forces withdrew down the Canongate. Even their retreat was beset with difficulties. One piece of the heavy ordnance sank in the muddy ground and took all night and a lot of effort to dig out.[6] On 21 October, Mar, like his predecessor, cut his losses and withdrew to Leith. Great was the disappointment to all those who had left the city in expectation of its capture in this second siege. The attackers had lost 100 men, the defenders sixteen. A war of attrition would be bloody and prolonged.

35 The Flodden Wall on the west side of the Pleasance.

News of Adam Gordon's victory over the Forbes at Tulliangus on 17 October in the North raised the spirits of the Castilians and depressed those of their enemies in equal degree, and his burning of the tower of Towie with thirty-seven souls inside was further evidence of the brutality of the war. Mar dispatched 200 soldiers under the Master of Forbes to curb the Gordons, and Grange sent a unit of harquebusiers by sea to reinforce Adam. At Crabstone the two armies met, and again the Queen's was victorious. Adam thought 'now to play the King... and rules all the north, at present, as he pleases,' bemoaned Bannatyne, 'God shorten his time.'[7]

In their military endeavours in the north and south the King's party had failed and appealed again to England. This time Elizabeth was obliged by events to commit herself further than her natural instincts urged. She decided to put her cousin Henry Carey, Lord Hunsdon, the Governor of Berwick in charge. He was a rough impatient soldier rather than a diplomat, and was under strict instructions to work with his subordinate Drury – whose currency was at an all-time low – to put an end to the expensive civil war. 'For the accomplishing thereof there are but two means: the first by treaty, the next by force. The first is best.' Elizabeth was still determined only to get directly involved if all else failed. While offering generous terms to the Castilians, Hunsdon was to consider whether the Regent, subsidised and supplied by her, could take the Castle alone. She would rather finance the campaign than risk the lives of her own subjects.[8]

On behalf of the Regent, Morton was detailed to go to Berwick and apprise Hunsdon of the realities. For the belligerent Morton the reduction of the Castle was vital 'that the root of the troubles once plucked up, the branches may the sooner be cut away.' The ideal time to strike was before succour could arrive from France. He optimistically asserted that the town was without food, fuel or cash. One side was 'unwalled' – a bit of an exaggeration – and even the frost-hardened ground was a virtue, providing ideal conditions for an assault. He correctly asserted that once the town was taken, the lot of those in the Castle would be insupportable and they would be exposed to the extremities of the weather high up on their rock. He told the Governor that without English assistance the Regent could not take the town let alone the Castle. This time it was a further 3,000 foot and 200 horse they wanted as well as twelve siege cannon and all their appurtenances. Hunsdon did not trust or even like Morton and his party, but he saw the force of the arguments.

The Castilians on the other hand exasperated him with their naivety and unrealistic demands. Andrew Melville on their behalf suggested a joint rule of Mary and James, and a joint council equally divided between the two parties.

Henry Carey
Lord Hunsdon

MARK GERARDS.

ÆTATIS SVÆ 66
ANᵉ 1591

36 Henry Carey, 1st Lord Hunsdon, the English Commander-in-Chief.

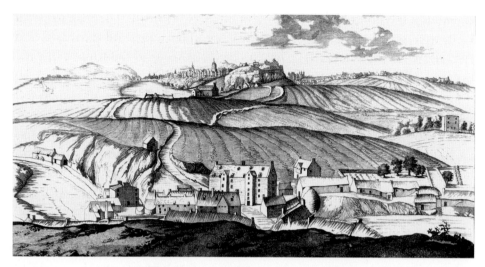

37 The prospect of Edinburgh from the Dean.

Hunsdon was amazed that they were still demanding what they knew would not be granted, the restoration of their Queen. 'If they think to alter Her Majesty they will be deceived.' Their intransigence convinced him that until a show of English force was actually made the Castilians would not enter into sensible negotiations, and so he began a campaign to force his Queen into action. The time was almost overripe, since the loyal Scots troops were ready to desert for lack of pay and the Castilians were buoyed up with hope of French aid in the spring. He warned her of the importance of securing Edinburgh before the French or Spanish got ensconced in Scotland with the Castle as their headquarters. The Regent's men could not reduce the Castle on their own. Money given directly to the Scots was money thrown away, and he would not like to risk good English ordnance to their charge. English troops had to be sent if only to secure her investment. With a mere 4,000 men for a month or six weeks at the most he could reduce the Castle and the whole kingdom. To avoid risk – and save coin – the ordnance could be dragged by a 100-strong team of cart horses rather than sent by sea. The expense of a short sharp campaign would not be exorbitant and any munitions left over could be returned to England. As a sweetener the Scots were at last offering to hand over Northumberland and the other rebels.[9]

While Elizabeth dithered a stand-off prevailed. The brute strength the Regent could muster had proved inadequate to take town or Castle. Starving them out was the next expedient to try. All commerce with the traitors had to be prevented. Edinburgh was outlawed. All the administrative processes of the crown and the courts of justice were transferred to Leith. The magistrates at Leith were given powers to search all imports and exports. All those who had left Edinburgh were ordered to take an oath of loyalty to the King, while the names of all those bearing arms or assisting the Castilians were published in the principal burghs and ports so that their embarkation could be prevented and their goods confiscated.[10]

Yet it was an odd sort of civil war. The blockade was porous. Prisoners openly walked in the streets of Leith and the Regent granted licences to burgesses to return home to fetch their goods. When Mar realised that these licences were being used as a cover of continuing trafficking with the beleaguered town, they were withdrawn, and Morton issued orders that all prisoners be detained in close custody.[11] But a complete economic blockade was beyond the power of the Jacobeans. A raiding party rustled Morton's sheep from under his nose, and when he huffily demanded them back Grange replied that he wished there had been more.[12]

Given that the Castilians had to send out marauding parties to replenish their supplies, violent encounters were surprisingly few and far between. On Monday 10 December the first serious skirmish for two months took place. A party of Castilians were awaiting at Boroughmuir the arrival of victuals and coal when a large detachment of the Regent's men came upon them. Several of the Castilians were killed, and over fifty taken prisoner including their best

38 The south side of the Castle, a good vantage point for a cannonade.

91

captain, James Haggerston, 'again.' The rest fled within the Kirk o' Field Port hotly pursued by Captain Mitchell, Keeper of Holyrood, who for his bravado, was badly wounded and taken prisoner with six or seven of his troops. Other than those the Leith forces lost not a man. Golfers were not so fortunate. On 23 December horsemen from the castle came across some burgesses playing on the Leith links. They invited them back to Edinburgh and slew three of them who proved reluctant to relinquish their game.[13]

So ended the first full frustrating year of the war. Grange defiantly held the principal city and strongest Castle in the kingdom. The Gordons held the north. Lord Semple had been defeated in the west. Fernihurst had carried all before him in the south. The only resolution Elizabeth seemed to show was in refusing to send any force to reduce the Castle and even if she were to do so, Mar feared it could still hold out. The Regent began to grow colder in the quarrel and withdrew himself to Stirling, alleging that he could see nothing but the wreck of the country by those purporting to fight for King or Queen but in reality 'pushed only by their own partialities of ambition, greediness and vengeance, England kindling up both parties and then laughing them all to scorn.'[14]

Yet despite Mar's despair the *raison d'être* of the Marian cause was fast diminishing. With the English parliament demanding the Scottish Queen's head after the discovery in November of another conspiracy to depose Elizabeth and replace her with Mary – the Ridolphi plot – there was virtually no prospect of her return. There was also a strong stench that Mary's failings and delinquencies were only all too real and were continuing. The King's party could portray the growing James as the rising sun to Mary's falling star. Without prospect of the Queen's return to Scotland those committed to her forlorn cause continued to ebb away.

9

DIVIDED IN MINDS
January 1572 to July 1572

'Hereafter the civil wars began at sik rigour that ilk man drew to a
faction, some for the King and others for the Queen... the son against
the father, and brother against brother; some for mere defence of lawful
powers, others for gain... and the inhabitants of the good town were so
divided in minds that they spared not to come against other in open
hostility, as it had been against a foreign and auld enemy.'[1]

'The Earl of Morton – who rules the Regent – will never agree to
accord but with such conditions as the contrary party will never grant.'
Lord Hunsdon[2]

In the very cold, bleak days of January 1572 when no military action of any
sort could be contemplated, protracted peace negotiations between the various
parties took place. Queen Elizabeth still resisted all attempts to induce the
English into violent confrontation with the Castilians. While hope remained
that they might come to an accord she could not be induced to use force. The
French too joined the chorus urging an abstinence and concord.[3] Meanwhile
both sides, worn down and worn out, seemed agreeable to a grudging truce.
The Scylla and Charybdis on which the venture foundered were the obduracy
of the King's party stiffened by Morton's dominance, and the over-confidence
of the Castilians who, seeing no English assistance for their rivals and knowing
of Mar's despondency, were prepared to demand too much.

First the English laid down their proposals for Scotland. Elizabeth should be
the conservatrix of the whole accord and both sides should make their pledges
before her. There could be no question of the restoration of Mary, and the
accession of James VI and the regency of Mar must be universally
acknowledged. The Regent should act in concert with a council of sixteen

members, the majority of who should be of the King's party. Lands and title and offices should be restored to all those forfeited, with the exception of those responsible for the murders of the two Regents. One final issue remained: who should hold the Castle? The English preference was for Grange to be paid off, but if he could not be induced to vacate his office they would settle for him holding it in the King's name with a garrison sufficient to protect his charge but not to launch attacks. He was defending Edinburgh not maintaining an army of occupation.

The Regent's party, naturally in large agreement with the main proposals, were not happy on this point but would just have to compromise, cognisant of their inability to capture the Castle on their own. Lethington and Grange were equally quick to lay out their position: a regency council equally appointed, Grange to hold Edinburgh Castle during the minority and full restitution of all forfeitures on both sides. Significantly there was no mention of a Regent.[4] To accept a regency was to accept the deposition of Mary and the accession of an infant King. This the Castilians would not do. Mary was still their Queen, but in exile.

As the blockade bit ever more deeply the Castilians were both provoked and compelled into ever greater depredations upon the surrounding estates of their enemies, depredations that were met by bloody counterattacks, and that merely increased the acrimony of the struggle. The first instance of the venom between Morton and Grange was evidenced by the tit for tat actions they took in February against each other's properties. In revenge for the ruination of his sister's wedding by the seizure of the venison and wine by a Castilian raiding party, Morton made for Grange's lands in Fife and burnt his house and all of his crops. While Morton was away, a large detachment issued from Edinburgh and sacked his town of Dalkeith, burning many of the houses, and taking such spoil as they could carry. His temptingly close lands and fat cattle were to be subjected to several other such pillaging raids by the Castilians. It was rightly observed that 'the burning, slaughter and spoil of the Earl of Morton's friends will be a great impediment to the peace, except that the parties spoiled and other injuries done be satisfied or revenge taken.' Retaliatory raids on Lethington's house at Thirlstane 'marvellously hardened them of the castle.'[5]

In early March, Captain Haggerston – free yet again – led a large raiding party out of Edinburgh to bring in livestock, but was intercepted by Methven and Ruthven at the Boroughmuir. After a brief skirmish the Castilians galloped for home. The young, impetuous Methven in hot pursuit came too close to the guns of the Castle, and was hit by a cannon ball the force of which severed his right arm, and decapitated his horse. He died imploring God for mercy. Seven of his men were also killed in a demonstration of just how deadly accurate cannon fire could be.[6]

Further afield violence proliferated. Cavalry sorties from the Castle despoiled Clydesdale, while the Hamiltons raided around Glasgow. When it was reported that Fernihurst had marched to burn Jedburgh, Mar sent troops to intercept them.[7] The Marians had got to within two miles of their prey when they realised that they were outnumbered and withdrew to Hawick. There the Regent's forces surprised them in an early morning raid. Fernihurst, on horseback, decided to save himself by deserting his men and was joined in this dubious manoeuvre by the aptly named Captain Trotter, his captain of harquebusiers. After a few shots had been fired and some horses had been killed the entire force surrendered and was taken prisoner to Jedburgh, the town they had aspired to destroy.

Elizabeth sent two emissaries – technically under Hunsdon's direction – to commend her compromise proposals to both sides. Randolph and Drury were sent back to Scotland, arriving in Edinburgh in mid-February. Under a magnificent armed escort they were ushered into Leith and to the council summoned for their coming. The English emissaries delivered Elizabeth's letters and, their contents digested, it was soon agreed that if the town of Edinburgh were thrown open a truce could be brokered. The English deputation, with a degree of optimism, then rode under light escort to the Castle. They were met half-way by another escort under Lord Seton, and by a dramatic cannonade of salutation from the ramparts high above. Sir James Melville met them at the first gate of the Castle, the constable at the second, and at the third Grange himself. They were led into the council chamber where were assembled virtually the entire Marian party: the Duke, Huntly and his brother Patrick, Galloway, Crichton of Dunkeld, Home, James Balfour, John Maitland, Fernihurst, Robert Melville and, sitting because of his infirmity, the old eminence grise, Lethington himself. After their missives were delivered, the emissaries urged the Marians to conclude a peace and save their country from further calamity. Lethington spoke first and for them all. They were agreeable to an abstinence, but on the point of allegiance to the King they wanted more time to consider how far they could yield in 'duty, conscience and honour.' Afterwards Drury saw Lethington alone, recognising that he was the key to the successful conclusion of the whole mission, while Randolph conferred with the titular leader, the Duke of Chatelherault. After the meeting the English left for Leith, somewhat despondent and with a sense of little achieved. Conferring later with his colleague, Drury delineated the gathering in a number of thumbnail sketches: 'The Duke continues still in his

39 Lord Seton, 'malicious, vain, despiteful' and his brood.

simplicity, the Earl of Huntly full of malice against his enemies, Lord Home led as Lethington lists; Lord Seton malicious, vain, despiteful – neither honest nor reasonable; two worthy prelates neither learned, wise nor honest; Fernihurst fretting and fuming for his last defeat – more proud than witty or reasonable; but generally all concluding that peace is best.' Randolph shared his distaste for the Castilians. He found 'more words they have spoken than deeds that have followed' and found 'small appearance of any good end.'[8]

As a fall-back to failure, Drury sent to Hunsdon for enough money to pay the soldiers of the King's party for two months. Hunsdon replied that no such sums were available but he could let them have £500 or 1,000 marks. Drury and Randolph pointed out the dangers of present parsimony especially as it was rumoured that Grange was about to pay his garrison. The King's party were in desperate financial straits. By March the recurrent monthly expenditure on the 7,000 soldiers based at Leith was over £4,500, and most of them were owed back -pay which amounted to over £20,000.[9] Parliament was forced to ratify the issue of a new coin, minted at Dalkeith, called the half merk piece (6s 8d), but its silver content was heavily debased and compared unfavourably with the outstanding Marian coinage being minted in the Castle by James Mossman and James Cockie. As a result of establishing a 'cunyie hous' [coining house or Mint] within the Castle in March, Mossman was dismissed from his official post as Royal Assay, and put to the horn by the King's party. Mossman, an elderly and important burgess whose father had, on James V's instructions, enclosed the crown of Scotland with arches, and his brother-in-law were risking not just their property and status but their very lives by coining for the Marians at a time when their party was already in decline. They were not even doing so from necessity since the money provided from France and from the Pope was largely in gold crowns which circulated freely in Scotland, but as a propaganda exercise, to keep in circulation good-quality Marian coins. They also minted counterfeit half merks in James' name in an attempt to undermine the coinage of the King's party. Drury sent a sample of this illicit coinage to Burghley – not for its value but for the novelty.[10]

Despite all their efforts, however, the Marians had even greater problems than their opponents. During the exceptionally harsh winter months the embargo was beginning to bite. Ships were ordered to unload at Leith, and forbidden to dock further up the Firth on pain of the confiscation of their goods and the hanging of their crew. To enforce the blockade Mar billeted 300 of Argyll's Highlanders in Craigmillar, Corstorphine, Craighall and Merchiston, each garrison being three miles from each other and two miles from Edinburgh. Morton's men stopped all suspect traffic, seizing coal from women bringing it to Edinburgh, and monitoring the Queen's Ferry. All trade with Edinburgh was forbidden on pain of branding on the cheek or hanging on the gibbet. This was no idle threat. Country folk who attempted to smuggle their little stores into the market were hanged, drowned or – if children – branded. On one occasion eleven young boys were cast in prison for carrying victuals to the besieged. Many poor women, bringing in food for their children and themselves rather than blockade breakers, were hanged, 'one heavy with child who gave birth upon the gallows, a cruelty not heard in any country.' Some were so desperate that they would smuggle fish 'between their legs,' and two men and a women were hanged for trying to bring leeks and salt into Edinburgh.[11] Yet nothing deterred them.

Civilians on both sides suffered almost equally. The inhabitants of the Canongate, the majority of whom were thought to be trading with the enemy, were evicted from their houses and moved to Leith as part of an attempt to draw a two-mile strip of no man's land around the town to prevent provisions being secreted into Edinburgh. In retaliation the Edinburgh authorities employed the notorious 'Captain of the Chimneys' to demolish the house of the Provost-in-exile, James MacGill, who became the first and most prominent victim of a notorious campaign that lasted five months. The properties of Nichola Todart, a merchant, and Michael Gilbert, a goldsmith, soon followed, a prelude to more. The authors of the *Diurnal* and the *Historie*, both of whom seemed to have been in the town throughout, attributed this to the need for fuel particularly after the King's forces had sabotaged the machinery of the coal pits around the town. As fuel grew scarcer, timber from the demolished houses was sold by stone weight for ever more exorbitant prices. This cannot alone explain the continuing destruction into mid-July. Venom played its part, as did blackmail, the demolition being designed to force the exiled burgesses to redeem their property. Drury claimed that the largest houses were being ransomed for up to 50,000 merks. These stern proceedings so terrified the neutral citizens that 100 of them fled to Leith, but instead of finding succour there they were perceived not as loyal King's men but, by their dalliance in Edinburgh, as potential fifth columnists or economic migrants. Those without the Regent's new licence required for residence were driven back to the capital under pain of death for adults or branding 'for bairns.' They returned to find the gates closed and their houses so much firewood.[12]

Thirty or more mills within four miles of Edinburgh were destroyed in early April, and on Saturday 6 April the Regent's men had the temerity to break five or six mills within cannon shot of the Castle. The artillery bombarded the breakers and a party from the Castle came out to engage them. The skirmish was fierce with several fatalities on both sides, including Mar's page boy. These provocations galvanised the Marians into an unsuccessful attempt to burn

40 Coins struck at Dalkeith and Edinburgh: examples of those struck for James VI's first coinage
are (top two rows, obverse and reverse) the Ryal (1570), two-thirds Ryal (1571), and one-third
Ryal (1571). Two examples of the poorly struck and debased coins of the 'second coinage' are
(bottom row) the Half Merk/Noble (1572) and Quarter-Merk/Half Noble (1572). It is impossible
to say whether they were struck officially at Dalkeith or counterfeited by the Marians
in the Castle.

down the mills around Leith. Unsurprisingly, dearth was accompanied by soaring grain prices. By June, oatmeal was sold in Edinburgh for 20 shillings a boll [48 gallons], malt was almost impossible to get and ale was priced out of the market at 16d a pint, the Castilians being forced to drink vinegar and water instead. The minting of base coin was another factor in price rises.[13]

The fruitless negotiations were still continuing, the English passing from one camp to the other, but being foiled by the irreconcilable aims of, and demands made by, each side. An impetus to the English endeavours, however, came from the Continent. On 27 March the Treaty of Blois had been signed between Elizabeth and Charles IX of France which included an article in which both pledged to try to negotiate a peace in Scotland. This was considered all the more vital to forestall any attempt by the Spanish to install themselves in Scotland. Letters had been intercepted from the increasingly desperate Mary to the Duke of Alva in which she gave herself and her realm into the protection of Spain. Seton, her returning emissary from Alva, had been driven by a storm into Harwich. Disguising himself as a mariner he eventually made his way to the Castle, but his papers and instructions had fallen into his enemies' hands. In them they found that he had assured Alva that with a small force he might seize the young King and spirit him away to Spain.[14] It proved fanciful, but it was a frightening prospect at the time. Elizabeth showed these documents to the French who were so appalled at the prospect of a Spanish hold on Scotland that, rather than rushing to aid the Marians themselves, they did a *volte-face* and ordered their ambassador to call upon the Castilians to acknowledge the King and make peace.

When it was rumoured that Grange and Lethington were beginning to fall out, hoping that dissent among the allies might lead to concessions, Randolph and Drury once more braved the lion in his den. He told them bluntly that the Queen had been forced to abdicate and so he could neither accept the King's authority, nor give validity to a Regent. The exchange was heated. Drury and Randolph conferred yet again with Mar, handed him copies of the castle's demands and asked him to consider them carefully. The two sets of proposals contained in two short documents included in the brief to Hunsdon, showed how irreconcilable the parties were.[15] Drury and Randolph were wearying of the task and wished to be recalled. They were making no headway by their efforts, and were bringing much opprobrium upon themselves. On Sunday 13 April while walking towards Leith, Drury was 'dribbed at' [shot at] by two harquebuses which missed him very narrowly.[16] Drury had nine lives it seemed, being fired at on eight separate occasions by soldiers from both sides. They were all either remarkably poor shots, or drunk, or they fired only in threat, for they all missed their target, though often felling innocent bystanders. Drury got sick of complaining, for his complaints came to nothing. 'Justice is dead on both sides,' he moaned. 'The magistrates of neither side dare punish a soldier for any offence he can commit.'[17]   He would 'sooner serve the Queen in Constantinople than among such inconstant and ingrate people.'

Two events proved further brakes to the stalling peace process. On 4 March the important keep of Blackness on the Firth of Fourth threw in its lot with Edinburgh, thereby endangering the navigation between Leith and Stirling, and greatly encouraging the Castilians. It was some consolation for the loss of Dumbarton and Grange soon augmented its garrison with twenty harquebusiers from Edinburgh to ensure that it did not fall to like subterfuge.

The other event, the first execution of combatants since the one-off killing of Huntly's garrison at Brechin in August 1570, brought about a series of tit for tat killings that stoked up bitter resentments on both sides. On Tuesday 15 April, four of Home's Borderers were taken by Morton's men and hanged at Leith. Presumably they were reivers, probably out rustling for the town, possibly out for a little private plunder, but they were punished for acts of war – their participation in the Stirling raid and the burning of Dalkeith. The four were soon avenged. After dinner the following day the Castilians convicted five prisoners including a servant of Morton, of treason for taking up arms against their Queen, and of the burning of Fernihurst's crops. They were hanged at the Mercat Cross. A sixth was to die as well, an officer named Bruce, but his kinsman was one of the Marian captains. He smuggled him out of the

41 Blackness Castle.

Netherbow Port and turned him loose to seek refuge in Leith. The Regent in turn ordered the summary execution of those prisoners held in Stirling and elsewhere.

On 23 April six of Captain Mitchell's men were put to death by men under the recently reprieved Captain Bruce who caught them drunk in the Canongate. Two days later Morton with a force of 300 horsemen lay in wait at Cramond for Lord Claud, whose arrival in Edinburgh with cattle rustled from around Glasgow and Paisley was imminently expected.[18] Morton's men were frustrated in this design when Claud did not appear, but took their spite out on a party of twenty soldiers from Captain Scoullar's troop, led by a lieutenant and sergeant, going from Edinburgh to Blackness. Fifteen of them, who had surrendered themselves and their weapons, were killed in cold blood, another dire decline in the conduct of the wars. The rest were driven to Leith like cattle, being beaten all the way with sticks, and goaded at spear point. They were hanged on a gigantic gibbet at Gallowlee in sight of the Castle. When criticised for this outrage by one of the Leith clergy, Morton had him tortured and strung up too. In retaliation, two prisoners were publicly and prominently hanged from the Castle walls in full view of the Regent's forces. The brutality was started by Morton and was continued by him. Bannatyne records that shortly after the hanging of the five there 'came a drum from Edinburgh to Leith, desiring that fair wars be used.' He records no reply nor response. Presumably there was none.[19]

In an incident at the end of May a party from the castle by their bravado lured some of the troops from Leith to attack them on the hill of Craggingate, and soundly repulsed them with considerable loss. A few days later in the early hours of Tuesday 3 June, word got to Leith that a party from the Castle was out scavenging, and a party of horse and foot was dispatched to surprise them. The main Castilian party had already retired into Edinburgh, although five scouts placed beyond the walls because of the mist were come upon unawares. Two were killed and one mortally wounded, the other two taken prisoner. They were hanged where they had lived, one at Musselburgh, the other at Tranent. The Castilians later that day came upon two non combatants from Leith and left them for dead. They tried to provoke another attack on their men while they kept to the Cragingate but this time the challenge was not taken up. A combination of a heatwave punctuated by torrential summer downpours seems to have doused the martial ardour of both sides for a time.[20]

The Castilians' garrisons in Niddrie, Blackness and Livingston still remained and served a vital role in the convoy of men and provisions and as bases for plundering raids. Each night in early June nearly 300 soldiers under Lord Seton left Edinburgh to provide armed escorts to convoy supplies coming into the capital.[21] By this means Lord Fleming, who had landed at Blackness, furnished the Castle with more money to pay the soldiers. It was to be his last trip. Shortly after his arrival he was wounded in the knee by a ricochet. The wound soured and two months later he was dead.

The Regent wanted to put a stop to this blockade running and gathered a squad of 300 men for the purpose. Some urged him to attack Edinburgh when so many of its defenders were away, but his men would not move until they were paid, and more cautious sentiment prevailed. Niddrie, the capital's main supply base was a safer bet. Having bribed one of the garrison to betray it, a party set out from Leith by night to take it by surprise. The surprise was to be on them. The traitor had betrayed them, and as they began to ascend their assault ladders, huge blocks of oak suspended from the battlements were released, crushing seventeen of them to death.[22] This affront could not go unchallenged. At 8 a.m. on 10 June Morton himself rode out from Leith with a large force of 200 horsemen and foot to besiege Niddrie. Getting wind of this movement four ensigns of foot and two culverins under Huntly took the opportunity to attack the garrison of Merchiston House, situated at the west end of the Boroughmuir, half a mile from the Castle. After two hours of battering it was about to surrender when help arrived. The Regent and his men stood barely 1,000 yards from the enemy. Although no fighting took place the Castilians withdrew from the siege and made off with their valuable ordnance to the Castle, the Regent in pursuit. He soon came within cannon shot. The Castilians rallied and took up position on the Craggingate. Mar stopped his forces at the foot and took cover in some quarry holes. The Castilians rushed down the hill at their enemies but the Regent stood his ground, rallied his troops and led a counter-charge which scattered the enemy forces. Huntly's horse was killed under him, his brother was shot in the foot, and Hugh Lauder, their sergeant-major, was shot in the thigh. They fled towards Edinburgh and took refuge behind the garden walls. About sixteen of their party had been killed when Mar called off the pursuit. Twenty-four others were taken prisoner, and the merchants of Leith petitioned the Regent that they should be executed. In deference to this request fifteen were tried, and six were hanged in the presence of their comrades. One of the condemned said that as Mary Queen of Scots had once given him life, now in her cause, he made just recompense with his death. Another, a sixty-year-old schoolmaster, as he stood on the scaffold declared that he had acted under duress, the Provost of Edinburgh having threatened to hang him if he did not join the raiding party. His protestation did not save him, nor did his years nor his profession. Hanged he was, alongside a former priest, William McKie.[23]

'This aforesaid cruelty,' laconically commented the *Diurnal*, 'tendit neither to God's glory nor good conscience as appeared.' Indeed it did not, and worse. The Castilians took revenge. Six prisoners were executed, the house of David Kinloch, who had been one of those who clamoured most loudly for harsh treatment, was demolished the next day and the young able-bodied apprentices and servants left behind by their masters to protect their property were rooted out.[24] The percipient Hunsdon, far away in Berwick, clearly recognised the obstacle to agreement that this escalation of violence posed, 'so that there are no prisoners to be taken on either side henceforth – but mortal wars.'[25] In contrast to his colleagues, however, Hunsdon repeatedly laid the blame squarely on Morton and others on the Regent's side whose malice towards the Castilians and material self-interest – they had 'tasted their adversaries' spoils' – was getting in the way of an agreement. In his opinion 'the ending of these controversies will never be by treaty, and the lack is rather on the King's side than the other, for their desire is only to bring the Castilians to appointment by force and not by treaty, not being minded to part with anything they have gotten nor to restore anything they posses.' A pacification, with a concomitant restitution of forfeited property, was very definitely not in their interest.[26]

Small acts of amnesty did take place – whether out of mercy or policy is open to debate. On 21 June the King's party, from a position of strength, and well aware that Edinburgh was on the verge of famine, offered a two-day truce during which all those within Edinburgh could remove themselves with their families, servants and chattels to the countryside. The Castilians' immediate response was to assemble everyone in the town, saying that they were free to go but promising those who stayed sufficient meat and money. It was mainly women and children who went, only to be relieved by the Regent's men of what possessions they carried. The men for the most part stayed put. From late June on, those remaining in the Burgh were confirmed Marians and the encumbrance of the women and children was largely removed.[27]

On Sunday 29 June the Regent's cousin, Patrick Home, was slain while attempting to engage a party from Edinburgh bringing in supplies. The next evening at 5 p.m. when a large raiding party set off from Edinburgh for Merchiston, a detachment of cavalry from Leith issued out to intercept them at the Boroughmuir while another party in a surprise attack approached the Abbey wall, near the park. In the meantime the remaining Castilian garrison retired to the Potterow and from there made for the West Port. A sturdy rearguard action by six men who turned and fired into the cavalry stayed their pursuers until the gates could be shut against them. Thus the Leith force just missed destroying the bulk of the town garrison, some 200 men.[28] Despite this setback, the Regent's forces clearly had the upper-hand.

At this vital juncture Mar was compelled to deplete his force around Edinburgh to deal with problems in the north. On Sunday 6 July with 1,600 men Adam Gordon had won a notable victory at Brechin. He then made for Montrose, extorting a ransom of £2,000 Scots and two tuns of wine out of its citizens, took Arbroath and Forfar, and seized the Laird of Dunne's house with its three or four field pieces.[29] This distraction, by deflecting troops north, effectually undermined all attempts at a comprehensive blockade of the capital. Another misfortune befell the King's party when the Laird of Arbroath defeated Captain Crawford in a skirmish in the woods around Hamilton. Crawford's assailants had formerly been in the service of the Regent and approached seemingly as friends. In the ensuing fracas some of Crawford's best men were killed, including Harry Wetherbourne, the first over the wall at Dumbarton. Others were taken prisoner, although Crawford escaped. Arbroath received a slight injury to his nose and his captain of horse was badly wounded. Whatever the actual losses on Crawford's side – thirty according to the Castilians, twelve if you believed Leith – it was a sorry defeat for one of the Regent's best generals. The Hamiltons then besieged Lord Semple in Hamilton Palace and church until a large relief force under the Provost of Glasgow compelled them to retire to Hamilton Castle.[30] Back at Edinburgh disaster was averted by the determined action of the Edinburgh Band, the militia led by Adam Fullerton which reached a peak of about forty per cent of the Regent's forces in July, successfully plugging the manpower gap made by these military efforts elsewhere.

Fitful negotiations, bedevilled by lack of trust, continued all this time between Drury and the Castilians. De Croc, the French ambassador, was also involved, encouraging the Castilians and adding to English fears that the Castilians were trying 'to cast a bone [of contention] between the French King and Elizabeth.'[31] An element of farce briefly erupted into the proceedings when the force of fire from empty cannon saluting the French legation to the Castle tossed pebbles into the dignitaries, killing one of them and wounding four others.[32] Nonetheless, the labours of the ambassadors of England and France were to pay off when at the end of July an 'abstinence' was signed with provisions to summon the estates of the realm to mediate a general peace which would secure the honour and safety of the Queen's supporters. The truce was to last for two months and the terms were simple: that the town of Edinburgh should no longer be a city under siege but open to all as it had been when the Regent Lennox left it on 27 January 1571, that the Castle be garrisoned with a force no greater than it had on that date, and that the French King and English Queen should arbitrate between the parties.[33]

The Castilians had not only initiated these peace overtures, but they agreed to relinquish control of the town and admit their enemies into their own backyard even though they fully appreciated that they were prejudicing themselves by 'putting out of their hands their chief security.'[34] Why? Necessity was the answer. Publicly, of course, they denied that they were in dire straits, professing that they were 'desirous of peace, that it may appear to the world that they are reasonable in all their dealings, and have no delight to nourish an ungodly flame of evil dissensions.' Privately they were well-aware that the conditions were disadvantageous and to save the Castle they had to relinquish the town. They had no choice. The latter was worn down, on the verge of starvation, and short of water and the reserves of the former were being exhausted on sustaining the townsfolk.[35] The Castilians were gambling for that elusive commodity that a truce would give them – time: time to re-provision, time to reorganise and replenish their forces, time for aid to arrive from either France or Spain, time to transform their fortunes and win the war. It was the only hope they had. De Croc had assured them that Charles IX would at least guarantee their security, or even at last intervene. His master's failure to live up to either hope would again demonstrate how disastrous Scottish dependency on France could be.

10

LED UPON THE ICE
August to November 1572

They compelled the inhabitants of the town to lay all armour from them, although
they themselves kept their swords all the day long during the abstinence, and
behaved themselves towards their neighbours rather like unto commanders and
masters than ordinary citizens.[1]

The huge reversal resulting from the abstinence was immediately brought
home to the Castilians. On Thursday 31 July, a few hours before the truce was
to begin, the exiles returned in force and in armour, parading with their
banner up the Canongate, led by their ministers, John Brand wearing his robes
and carrying a Bible, and John Durie in full armour with a caliver on his
shoulder and two dags [pistols] at his belt. They refused to wait until the
following day and entered Edinburgh preceded by a body of troops who stood
in an uneasy standoff with those Castilian soldiers still in the town. When
Brand was asked what their respective apparel meant, he replied, 'It means we
come to offer peace, which if ye refuse, ye shall have war.' It was the voice of
the Church militant and triumphant.[2] The Regent, a stickler for the letter of
the truce, did not make his entrance into Edinburgh until the morning of 1
August. He took 200 foot and some horsemen with him, precisely the same
number as Lennox had marched out with a year and a half before, thus
symbolically asserting his resumption of authority. Chatelherault, Huntly and
Seton meanwhile scuttled out of the town taking their troops with them.

On 2 August Morton was appointed Lord Lieutenant of Edinburgh, with
the task of seeing that the abstinence was observed, a task he interpreted as
ensuring that the Castilians did not break the conditions by continued coining
or by levying money. He enlisted a new company of soldiers and taxed the
people of Edinburgh to pay for it. Morton's men and citizen bands kept 'watch
and ward day and night' and kept close guard of the twin hubs of the town,

42 The infirm and ailing Knox being helped from St Giles to the Netherbow.

the Tolbooth and St Giles Kirk. They behaved like an occupying force in a town taken by storm. The troops were billeted in the houses of those poor inhabitants who had sided with the Castilians and their unwilling hosts were compelled to sustain them. Over the next six months Edinburgh Marians, great and small were forced to appear before the Kirk Session, bare-headed and in sackcloth, to confess their sins against their neighbours. Most had to pay fines to the King's party some of which went into the pocket of Morton.[3]

The old guard were back in power and the town of Edinburgh was firmly under their control. In demonstration of this, on Sunday 24 August John Knox returned to his former pulpit in St Giles. He had agreed to preach on the sole proviso that he would not be 'pressed in any way to temper his tongue, or cease to speak against the treasonable doings of the Castle.'[4] He did not disappoint. The irascible old prophet was now so feeble that he could scarcely stand alone and his voice was barely audible, yet he preached with the same vehemence and zeal that ever he did. He was a symbol of the great Protestant past and of its triumphant future.

Too late, the Castilians protested to the English that they had been foully betrayed and that the truce had not been intended to be a justification for the burgh being rendered into the hands of their enemies and guarded 'as ane town of war by their forces.' The French were too far away to intervene and the French ambassador, De Croc, too mild mannered and too dilatory to take up their cause effectively. Ironically they had to look to England for succour and Elizabeth, to give her due, did take up their complaints with Mar. The Regent counterclaimed to the English that the abuses by the Castilians were far worse than their own, namely murder, coining, and seizures of men and property 'all done since the abstinence began.' Soon the Queen, unsurprisingly, became 'so wearied with these Scottish matters that she desire[d] rather to be a looker on than a part player amongst them.'[5]

On the same day that Knox preached in St Giles, a devastating event took place in France which shattered the Anglo-French bipartisan approach to affairs in Scotland. This was the St Bartholomew's Day Massacre of 20,000 Huguenots, a murder spree sanctioned by the French King and rejoiced in by Catholic Europe. It was the sort of climactic event that completely backfired on its perpetrators. When the dreadful news reached Scotland, it scuppered any chance of rapprochement, and even Grange wavered in his adherence to Mary. The Regent's propaganda machine denounced 'the imminent dangers and conspiracies of the Papists.'[6] Catholics were not to be trusted to live in amity with their Protestant neighbours. The Castle, held by Grange for Mary, tainted with her ties of blood and marriage with the French monarchy, was a

Catholic coven and could disgorge bloody ruin on the unsuspecting Protestant populace of the town. Knox, literally on his last legs, decried the King of France as a 'cruel murderer and false traitor,' and told De Croc to convey the message that sentence was pronounced against his master in Scotland and that his name would remain an execration to posterity and none of his loins would inherit the kingdom. The ambassador demanded that the Regent silence the preacher, but the Regent quipped that he could not even stop the mouths of ministers denouncing himself let alone a foreign potentate. De Croc departed in impotent dudgeon and for a while he and the other emissaries were held in such ill-repute that they went in fear of their lives. St Batholomew had worked 'a great alienation of minds from putting any trust in the French Court.'[7] French moral support for the Castilians was now a liability, and any suggestion that Catholic troops might enter Scotland would be greeted with horror and terror by most of the lowland populace.

Elizabeth, clad in mourning for the victims of the massacre, was visibly shocked and inwardly scared. Catholics were the enemy within as well as without the realm. Mary Queen of Scots took on a terrible significance as the potential epicentre of conspiracy. All the more vital to settle Scotland, lest the religious turmoil there spin out of control and threaten the stability and security of its southern neighbour. Elizabeth dispatched Henry Killigrew, Burghley's nephew, to replace the unpopular and partisan Randolph as her envoy to Scotland and to ensure that this abstinence unlike the first, would not fizzle out. The new envoy was to hear the complaints of both sides and knock their heads together, all the more imperative given the recent events in France. They should unite to protect the King, preserve the realm in peace and resist foreign interference – other than her own. In return Elizabeth promised to protect Scotland as she would her own realm, which was precisely what the Castilians feared. When Killigrew arrived in Leith he found 'tokens of war' everywhere, but over estimated the strength of the Marians: 'The Duke has fortified himself at Hamilton, Huntly makes himself lord of the north, Fernihurst is increasing in strength.' The Castilians, he knew, would not budge on holding the Castle as a safeguard for their futures and without English support the Regent could never take it by force. Killigrew recognised that Lethington was the major stumbling block to a lasting settlement. Getting him to England was the only way to pacify Scotland, he concluded, and suggested that he retire to Bath for his health's sake. He persuaded Burghley, after a breach of two years, to recommence a friendly correspondence with his counterpart to smooth the way. Lethington responded graciously, glad to resume a valued friendship, but showed no inclination to leave the Castle let alone the country. Killigrew resorted to beseeching the Almighty to guide him through this labyrinth.[8]

The abstinence was again prolonged at English insistence, this time to 6 December. Tantalisingly an agreement was almost concluded, at least according to Sir James Melville's own account. The Regent had sent Melville into the Castle to assure them that the Regent understood, 'how we are led upon the ice, and that all good Scotsmen would fain agree and settle the state.' Melville reported back that Grange was prepared to accommodate the Regent, so long as the Queen was detained in England. If she were ever freed no doubt she and her son would come to an accommodation between themselves 'to which all honest and good subjects on both sides would hold hand.' The Castilians for their parts desired no one's land or goods, only liberty to enjoy their own livings in peace. Mar summoned his brother-in-law, Tullibardine, and in his presence and that of his lawyer, Clement Little, put his hand in Melville's and swore the peace.[9] Somehow, however, the final settlement could not quite be concluded. Killigrew despaired and doubted the Castilians' sincerity in negotiating. When it came to the pinch they always evaded a resolution, all to further delay. The renewed abstinence had been to their advantage in gaining more time. In his view the devoted Morton was the only man in Scotland whom the English should pay heed to, and in his uncompromising approach to the Castilians he was at utter and open odds with Mar. The dying Knox added his siren voice to that of Killigrew, warning the English to 'take heed how you believe them of the Castle, for sure they will deceive you and trust me, I know they seek nothing more than the ruin of your mistress, which they have been about of long time.'

Suddenly, on 28 October 1572, the Regent died. His death was a result of natural causes, but precipitated, some said, by disappointment 'because he loved peace and could not have it.'[10] On his deathbed he had accepted defeat and dictated a last letter to Elizabeth urging her to send an army and adequate artillery to reduce the Castle.[11] Mar, in the short time allotted him, had failed to end the civil war and the ensuing chaos. This fell to his able but far more ruthless successor, James Douglas, Earl of Morton, who was elected unopposed as Regent on Monday 24 November 1572, the second day of the week of national mourning for the St Bartholomew's Day massacre.

On the same day as Morton's election, John Knox died. During his final hours he had confided in David Lindsay, the minister of Leith, that Grange's soul was especially dear to him and that he would not have it perish, if he could save it, and begged him to:

> go to yonder man in the Castle whom you know I have loved so dearly, and
> tell him that I have sent you yet once more to warn him, in the name of God,
> to leave that evil cause... neither the craggy rock in which he miserably

confides, nor the carnal prudence of that man [Lethington] whom he esteems a demi-god, nor the assistance of strangers, shall preserve him; but he shall be disgracefully dragged from his nest to punishment and hung on a gallows against the face of the sun, unless he speedily amend his life and flee to the mercy of God.[12]

This deathbed admonition the minister took to the Castle. Grange seemed at first to relent, but having consulted with Lethington, he returned and retorted angrily. Lethington added a word of his own for Knox whose special relationship with the Almighty moved the Secretary to mirth: 'go, tell Mr Knox that he is but a drytting [defecating] prophet.' This response and Grange's rejection were reported to Knox who continued to pray for him, trusting that his soul should be saved though his body should come to a miserable end. Two days after his death Knox was buried in St Giles' churchyard, being carried there in solemn procession by the new Regent and his lords. The great Reformer was dead but his powerful acolytes would carry his work to completion and his words would live on.

MORTON'S MANOEUVRES
November and December 1572

I fear the decay of alliance shall also decay other friendship, which may
do harm. Na things are more dangerous in this waltering and confusit
state nor is disdain and want of affability.
Alexander Hay[1]

The King ought not in any manner to suffer that this realm be reduced
altogether to devotion of the Queen of England for the consequence
which depends on it, which will be, without doubt, if the Earl of Morton
and his adherents, who are already rendered slaves of the said Queen, are
able to make themselves masters of this place.
Grange and Lethington[2]

The Regent Morton had strong support and was a strong man, a typical
Douglas, accustomed to command and without scruple. 'This Regent is a
shrewd fellow,' commented Killigrew. He would prove a longer lived and more
determined ruler than his predecessors. He rose in the esteem of his peers,
many of whom had suspected or resented his ambitions. To the Castilians he
was anathema. He started with a major advantage. As a direct result of the
murderous events in France, England, whose paranoia was not without reason,
became even more determined to prevent a Catholic resurgence on her
northern border. Consequently, Morton and the Protestants had the unusually
active backing of a near and powerful neighbour.

Initially Morton moved softly. His long-term policy was to divide and
conquer and his first aim was to regain the Castle. Grange, he feared, would
be the main obstacle, 'the instrument of the beginning and the continuance of
the troubles.' By holding onto the Castle and by his attempts to dictate

conditions Grange had 'passed the bounds of a subject.' The Regent was particularly incensed by the continued coining which had contravened, in his mind, the spirit of the abstinence.[3] Nonetheless he enlisted Melville to help in persuading the Castilians to go forward with him as they had been minded to do with Mar. Morton may have been moved to negotiate by a letter from Lethington sent to him when he was lying seriously ill, and reminding him of their past friendship and the many benefits that the Secretary had secured him. But it was more likely a bluff to camouflage his doings elsewhere. He assured Melville 'that none of the former Regents had at any time been more willing than he was presently to put an end to the civil troubles.' Let bygones be bygones. The Regent would not seek personal revenge 'but whoever would serve the King and be his friend, he would embrace.' He was willing to give whatever conditions the Earl of Mar had offered, or better. Melville would get the priory of Pittenweem, Grange the bishopric of St Andrews and the castle of Blackness; and everyone in the Castle would be restored to their lands and possessions. Melville acted as go-between conveying these and counter-proposals back and forth from the Castle. Grange was willing to agree and, after some reluctance, so too were Lethington and Home.[4]

The negotiations foundered on one decisive point. Grange wanted to bring the entire Marian party into the settlement, but Morton told Melville that his aim was to divide the Marians, not reconcile with all of them. If all were included they would one day unite and usurp him. Morton wished to punish some and pardon others, and would rather the punishment befell the Hamiltons and Huntly than the Castilians. Grange and Lethington were given the stark choice: either they must desert their friends or live with their integrity intact but under the threat that their friends might be induced to desert them. Grange was uncompromising. He could not be party to a betrayal. He replied that 'he had rather that they should leave and deceive him, than that he should do it unto them.' Morton seemed to admire this response of a man standing stiff upon his honesty and reputation, but immediately made overtures to the other Marians – Huntly and the Hamiltons in particular – offering them pacification. He enlisted Argyll to encourage his erstwhile confederates to see sense and summoned a parliament, which had to meet in a house protected by a barricade from fire from the Castle, to sanction an amnesty to those implicated in the murders of Darnley or Lennox, an amnesty which would reconcile their adversaries to the inevitable accommodation with the government. Morton concurrently decided to harry his foes into submission. Huntly's lands had already been forfeited for treason but Morton became vigorous in his pursuit of them. Lachlan Macintosh, for instance, was

43 Reconstruction of Edinburgh Castle in 1573, incorporating archaeological evidence
uncovered in the Yeoman-Driscoll excavations on the outer gate and entrance, and of a double
earthwork rampart. This is the sight that would have greeted the arriving English army.
St Margaret's Well can be seen on the right-hand side of the picture.

allowed to keep the lands granted him by the rebel Earl, but had to swear
allegiance for them to the Crown.[5] Drip by drip these factors were beginning
to have an effect.

But the final outcome was not yet certain. To establish firm government
and utterly subdue the King's enemies Morton must reduce Edinburgh Castle
and excise the cancer at the heart of the kingdom, the defiance of its garrison
and governor.[6] But how? They were increasingly isolated but remained
resolute. He lacked both the ordnance to batter down the Castle walls and the
troops to storm its defences, and those he had were half-mutinous for want of

44 A sixteenth-century cannon.

pay. To starve out the Castilians would be a laborious process since they had supplies for a year and could still come and go by the West Port, which was not guarded for lack of men. Their spies were still abroad and armed sorties could still launch attacks from the Castle. They could not retake the town, but safe in their shell they could take leisurely pot shots at its inhabitants. Parliament could still not be safely held in Edinburgh. The Castilians were unshaken, still confident in the strength of their fortress. Their chief fear was that England would eventually aid the Regent with men and munitions. Their chief regret was that France did not intervene while still it could, decisively on the side of the Marians. To France they continued to appeal for help.[7] France might yet intervene, and England might not.

Elizabeth continued to press for an accord. On 6 December the abstinence was again extended at English insistence to the 1 January in the express hope that reasonable peace conditions could be agreed. Killigrew went to Perth to meet Huntly and Athol, but the former failed to turn up, and the latter, while appearing pliant, wanted a further prolongation of the abstinence and continued negotiations with the Castilians.[8] When Killigrew appraised Morton of these requests the Regent was surprisingly agreeable, but on condition that the Castilians nominate three plenipotentiaries to negotiate a lasting peace; that any remaining differences be put to independent arbitration; that the coiners and their coining irons be removed from the Castle; that prisoners on both sides be freed, and that the castle garrison should subsist on normal daily rations and provisions and not stockpile supplies or munitions. On this basis a lasting peace might be possible. Killigrew went up with these stipulations to the Castle. The Castilians were willing to nominate commissioners and release prisoners, but said nothing of the sticking clause, the provision for the castle.

That very night Killigrew reported back to the Regent who eagerly concluded that all this prevarication was to allow time for aid to come from France. In vain, the ambassador urged that his Queen was still eager for peace. Morton exploded. He had taken on the government in the firm belief in English support. If it was not forthcoming and he was left in the mire he would quit his office. Killigrew tried to mollify him but urged that the best service he could do Elizabeth was to maintain the peace. Morton argued that while peace was most desirable, five months of truce had already passed and they were no nearer peace than when the abstinence first began. During this time the Castilians had provisioned the castle, and maintained their military forces to the prejudice of the King and his government. No further abstinence could be granted unless peace was assured. Otherwise the Castilians would wax and the King's party wane.

Once again Killigrew went to the Castle. The Castilians immediately rejected the condition of limited provisions for the Castle and refused to discuss the other demands before that matter was conceded. Unless they had free ingress and egress to the Castle they would have no truce. The abstinence would not be renewed again. Killigrew accepted the inevitable and withdrew himself to Leith not wishing to be caught up as siding in a war. Morton had played his hand well. He had not rejected a further abstinence out of hand, but had forced the Castilians to reject his terms and so bear the responsibility for its lapse. The Regent hoped that their intransigence would galvanise the English and alienate Huntly and the Duke.[9] It did both.

SHOT   HALBERDIER   PIKEMAN   LIGHT HORSE   HEAVY HORSE

45 Assorted infantrymen and cavalrymen of the period.

Regint Morton
1577

NEC TEMERE
NEC TIMIDE.

46 The Regent Morton, 'a shrewd fellow', 1577.

SAFE FROM NO MAN'S CURSING
January 1573 to April 1573

As long as the Castle holds out there will be trouble and treason among
them.
The Regent Morton[1]

I am at my wits end to consider [the Castilians'] case and fear their hearts
be hardened to an ill destiny.
Killigrew[2]

The truce ended with a single warning shot from the fortress at 6 a.m. on
Saturday 1 January 1573. The Castle then again began to send volleys through
the darkness of the winter morning.

The strong point nearest the Castle was St Giles Kirk where Morton had
placed his own small artillery on its fortified steeple. Peeping exposed above
the turf rampart, the steeple was a tempting target and initially it received more
attention than any other, but to little effect. On 2 January as the Sunday
morning sermon ended the castle fired eight cannon balls at the steeple but did
no harm to anyone in the church, although a nearby chimney was hit and two
bystanders were killed and two others hurt. An attempt to improve their
success rate was thwarted when a soldier sent out from the Castle to spy on
Morton's positions was captured and put to death.[3]

Over the coming days most of the fire was directed against the newly
erected Fish Market just west of the Mercat Cross. Some of the cannon balls
landed among the creels and baskets, and beat them into the air, scattering the
fish on the tops of some of the tallest houses. Regardless of the danger a
number of poor people employed themselves in gathering what they could
pick up. Five were killed in the process and twenty others injured.[4] A herald
from the Castle walls duly warned all the Queen's true subjects, 'wives and

47 Prospect of the Castle and city from the Nor Loch.

bairns' to leave the city before 15 January and boldly commanded Morton to surrender himself to the Castle authorities on that date. If the Castilians' sense of reality had left them their sense of regality had not.

Because those living, working or attending church in the High Street were vulnerable to casual fire from the Castle, the Regent ordered the recently appointed Provost, Lord Lindsay, to erect three traverses – dikes and ramparts of earth, turf and dung – across the street. They were so constructed as to afford considerable protection from gun shot and were so high as to deprive the Castilians of a clear and unobstructed view of the thoroughfare. One was raised near the Lawnmarket in front of the Tolbooth, and the other two at a proportionate distance from each other closer to the Castle and protecting the church. Although these defences were breached or bypassed by a number of ransacking and pillaging raids into the heart of the town by 'Castle folk who have greater liberty than is seemly,' they were never destroyed. The barricades transformed life in the Burgh to such an extent that on 13 January the Regent held the first parliament in the Tolbooth since the troubles began, although he still had to use replica regalia. Although eighty-seven great shot were fired from cannon and culverin at them 'for their welcome and salutation,' the only casualty was a 'poor dog killed before the Regent's door.'[5]

The town was protected. The next task was to reduce the Castle. Detailed planning was necessary for such an enterprise and English expertise was now at hand. The surveyor of Berwick, Rowland Johnson and John Fleming, his master gunner spent eight days in Edinburgh drawing up a detailed 'platte' or ground plan of the town and Castle. Their report was sanguine. Fleming told Killigrew that he would wager his life that with twelve cannon and six sakers he could beat down the Castle in a three-day bombardment. The batteries could be placed in two safe places and provide a devastating crossfire. But the Regent did not have twelve cannon and six sakers. It was cannon that the Regent lacked, not men, though he would have liked both and some money too. Killigrew asked him to make ready the only two culverins they had, one of which was at Tantallon, the other at Stirling. He was also to prepare some small field pieces to guard the trenches, and to provide for 'mandes' (mounds) for the battery. There would be no need for mines if a battery were constructed but a miner should be sent 'as a terror.' Pioneers, some horse and 300 footmen were also needed. The lairds and tenants of East Lothian were commissioned 'to cut and prepare certain rys [brushwood] and brume' to make gun emplacements for the ordnance.[6]

It all seemed too good to be true, and Elizabeth insisted on a second opinion. Captain Nicholas Errington, the Provost Marshall in command of the artillery, was dispatched north. He was a man who knew the Castle inside and out and was best able to report back to Burghley on its weaknesses and strengths, since his judgement was more reliable than that of the less experienced Johnson and Fleming. Killigrew and Drury both thought he should be the master of ordnance during the siege since he would know best how to place it. Errington concurred in the previous diagnosis, commenting both on the very mild winter and the ideal conditions for a siege. The English government began to plan for the inevitable. Thirty good English Shire horses would suffice – better than a 100 Scottish horse – to drag the ordnance from Leith. Planks for this were to be provided at Newcastle along with four hoys for transporting the ordnance, one barque or pinnace, and powder and tools. 1,000 soldiers and 200 pioneers and gunners were to be levied in the north.[7]

While these preparations were proceeding, the only measures Morton could take to 'pull this thorn out of his foot' were to deprive the Castilians of food and water and contact with the outside world. Utilising the English survey, he circled the Castle with a trench. The trenchworks also enveloped the water on the south-east side of the Castle, and Morton even drained the ditches to prevent this source of water being utilised. Crawford and Captain Home were posted to prevent the Castilians coming out the Castle gate. Instead, by

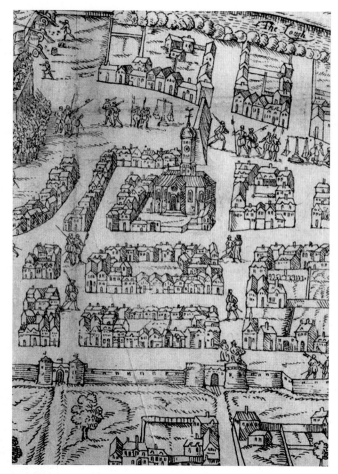

48 Detail of the siege, showing the traverses or barricades constructed in the High Street.

slipping out of a postern in the north side of the Castle, they managed to bring back water from St Margaret's Well. When Captain Brickwell spotted them the Regent ordered that the West Port be held against them and that they be deprived of the well. Captain Mitchell was stationed to intercept them at St Cuthbert's Kirk north-west of the Castle Rock, but he soon found a surer way: he poisoned the well with white arsenic, lime stones and fresh carrion. The Fore Well and three cisterns in David's Tower were the only water supply left. Ammunition in the Castle was also running low and things in general were getting desperate. Lethington too was waning. To his other ailments was added shell shock. When the great ordnance was fired he had to be carried into the low vault of David's Tower because 'he could not abide the shot.'[8]

In their desperation the Castilians, blind to reality, still buoyed up their hopes with hollow rumours that French troops were about to be dispatched and a confederacy of the Pope, Emperor, France and Spain was about to be formed to attack the Scots and English Protestants in favour of Mary Queen of Scots. They clung desperately to the hope of French rescue and the strength of their walls. All that did come was a French pinnace carrying the Scottish flag and Sir James Kirkcaldy, bringing 'small supply of monies' from Mary's dowry, and 'large promises' from the French King. Knowing that Edinburgh was closely guarded he disembarked at Blackness on 26 January. By bad luck the following day Morton enclosed it from the land side with a small force of only sixty horsemen and sixty foot.[9] It was enough. Without succour, on 3 February, Blackness fell to starvation. In those days of transient loyalties, the Governor, Alexander Stewart, was kept in post, and Kirkcaldy was imprisoned in the very place he had sought sanctuary. A few days later, when the Governor was absent, Kirkcaldy bribed the impoverished garrison and subverted them to their former allegiance. When the unsuspecting Governor returned he was clapped in irons. Needs must – he, in turn, bribed some of the soldiers to set him free, and with their help sprung a trap on Kirkcaldy. While he and his wife

49 The view of fire down Castlehill.

50 Gun loop in David's Tower, looking towards St Giles.

were being escorted to the gates by some of the garrison, others closed the iron yett behind them, trapping them between the two gates. Captain Lambie and his men were waiting outside for the signal to enter. When it was given Lambie entered the Castle, and James Kirkcaldy and his 15,000 francs were taken. He was brought to Edinburgh and committed to prison, from where he was to emerge only in August when he was to accompany his older brother to the scaffold. 'Thus God uses them that follow so good a mistress as the Castilians,' muttered Killigrew.[10]

For the present the Castilians could still make the occasional foray. On a stormy 4 February a party sallied out at twilight, surprised the trench guards, wounded half a dozen of them, and killed a boy before retiring. On the 7 February St Giles was attacked. On the 12 February, Grange launched another night attack on the trenches. After some fighting he managed to cross the barriers and set fire to some of the houses on the Castle Wynd and further down in Portsburgh. The wind was strong that night and the flames engulfed the wood and thatch and began to spread through the narrow streets. When attempts were made to quench them Grange made himself even more detested by firing the Castle's guns at those trying to douse the flames. As a result the fire raged unopposed from the ruined chapel of St Mary at the extremity of the Portsburgh, to that of St Magdalene, nearly a mile distant, burning itself out before Foster's Wynd. Although there were no injuries as a result of this act of vandalism there were some 100 houses burnt to the ground, and many salvaged items were looted by the soldiers – though whether they were Grange's or Morton's is not said. If Grange had hoped to clear Edinburgh of his enemies by this one drastic action he had failed. These escapades were themselves the dying embers of a fire flickering, and were to keep up morale among his own men as much as to inflict damage on the enemy. But there is the feeling that by such acts of 'causeless cruelty' the Castilians, knowing their days were numbered, were intent on inflicting as much suffering on others as would shortly be inflicted on them. Brutally pointless actions, such as these, alienated rather than intimidated the inhabitants of the Burgh, and a broadly dispassionate contemporary, the author of the *Historie of James Sext*, bluntly concluded that they 'wrought na good effect in the end, for not only the people that favoured [Grange] afore, and those who were his perpetual enemies, so cried out with maledictions, that he was safe fra no man's cursing.'[11]

By mid-February the English were sanguine. Verac, the face of France in Scotland, driven by a storm to land at Scarborough on his way to Aberdeen, had been detained,[12] Balfour had defected, Fernihurst's followers had surrendered, and Huntly and the Duke were on the verge of accord. On 23 February 1573, the eve of the expiry of the truce applying to them, realizing that their position was hopeless and that, with the intervention of England, the Castle would fall, the Duke and all his Hamiltons, Huntly, Ruthven, and Montrose were induced to sign another 'abstinence' known as the Pacification of Perth, by which they promised adherence to the Reformed Faith, recognised the King and the regency government, disbanded their troops, and handed over prisoners. In return all the acts of forfeiture against them were declared void. Their example was speedily followed by the submission of Buccleugh and many other of the lesser Marian nobility. Queen Mary would not return. King James would soon rule in his own right. Better to accept the inevitable, welcome the prosperity which would come with peace and maintain the traditional authority each magnate had long enjoyed in his domains. The Pacification of Perth was not so much a defeat or surrender on the part of the Marians as acquiescence in the inevitable and an accommodation with the government which they could not overthrow and with which they had to live. It was also an act of the utmost betrayal. The aristocracy had caved in and sacrificed Grange and Lethington to save their own skins. They looked too for pensions from Elizabeth, a necessary bounty to keep them on side and out of the pockets of their erstwhile paymaster, France. They wrote to Grange, lamenting that the straits to which they were reduced had compelled them to accept the agreement which the Regent had offered them, and thanking him for his help which they would never forget. This was the recompense, observed Melville, 'this good gentleman obtained for the great help, hazzard, and charges done and made for these lords.' Huntly completely accommodated himself with his new friends and sneered at those in the Castle. 'For myself,' he smugly asserted, 'I will mell no further in their causes than my lord Regent thinks expedient.'[13]

This surrender was a devastating blow from which there could be no recovery. Killigrew commented: 'And now there remaineth but the Castle to make the King universally obeyed, and this realm united, which peradventure, may be done without force after the accord; notwithstanding it standeth more reason and policy for her Majesty to hasten the aid rather now than before this conference.'[14] The English fully expected the Castilians to cave in – any rational man would in the circumstances. Yet when the aristocrats had all deserted their Queen, a solitary soldier and a decrepit civil servant held out in splendid – or squalid – isolation. Their defiance was impressive and heroic, a final reminder of the power Mary Queen of Scots could still inspire in her followers. Yet their resistance was futile, even puerile. And the Castilians must have known it, unless cocooned in their own little world they still dreamed dreams.

Their outside intelligence sources had now concluded a peace, their own spies and messengers were regularly discovered, and letters to and from the castle intercepted. When James Kirkcaldy had been taken prisoner the castle feared that their cipher had fallen into the hands of their enemies, and so changed it to that of John Chisholm. It did not put off the English cryptographers.[15] Sometimes arrows fell short, sometimes messenger boys were caught. The latter usually paid a heavy price for his service. When a cipher letter from Verac was found the youth carrying it was hanged. Other means of communication were thwarted or corrupted. A boy in the service of Grange was lured out of the Castle by his father whom the Regent had frightened into assisting in a little subversion. After an audience with Morton the youth agreed to carry on with his errands, but to deliver all the correspondence to the authorities. After a while the father, mother and son 'were taken for saving of their honesty', and so this intelligence was cut off. When the boy told his captors that Lord Seton, Lady Livingston and Athol were the conveyors of the letters and the persons most trusted by the Castilians, Morton summoned them to appear before him to renounce their allegiance. Resistance within the Castle precincts began to haemorrhage. Even Robert Kirkcaldy, the porter, deserted his post and threw himself on the Regent's mercy.[16]

The inevitable collapse of the Castilians was apparent to the Regent and he was now determined to accept no surrender but take the Castle by storm and punish its obdurate leaders whose greatest sins – firing on churchgoers and arson – had put them beyond the pale. Drury was equally convinced that only force would bring the rebels to heel and that it was vital Killigrew shared this opinion: 'If this castle be not recovered, and that with expedition, I see, methinks, the beginning of sorrows, and Her Majesty's peaceable reign hitherto decaying as it were in post, which God of his mercy defend.' Elizabeth could not escape these alarming arguments, and orders were sent to Drury to have everything ready to dispatch the army and the ordnance at a moment's notice.[17] Finally in March the first English troops arrived in Edinburgh in the shape of 100 pioneers who broke ground on Castlehill and formed a battery. They endured considerable loss until on the 15 March Grange attacked, drove them from their trenches and destroyed the fruits of their labour.

The English, who would have to pay for it in men and money, were still prepared to make more efforts to avoid a siege. During a lull Captain Errington went to the Castle to offer a surrender. In response the Castilians, as always, were content to pledge allegiance to the King but not to deliver the Castle. Errington reported back their distrust of the Regent and their fear that the English ambassador was partial to the other side. In the meantime they were fortifying the Castle as best they could. They lacked earth – vital in absorbing cannon fire – and had to make do with planks and timber, a poor substitute. They could get water but it was fit only for the launderer. Errington observed that although the place was strong, 'they are become desperate, [but] their hope of France is great.' He feared that they were prepared to die rather than yield 'to save their honours which they stand not little upon.'[18]

But still Elizabeth wavered over the cost, was fearful of success, and insistent that Morton do his own dirty work. Killigrew was in despair. He wrote that if the expedition were abandoned Scotland would be lost to them and united in a league with France. Every effort, she was assured, had been made to redeem the situation without using her forces, but the Castle remained and while it did the kingdom and King were not secure. Back he was sent to the Regent. Killigrew suggested that perhaps Lethington and Grange should be allowed to keep the Castle for the King. Morton was amazed at this suggestion and rejected it completely. Killigrew then proposed that at least they be granted the same personal security as had the other lords. Morton at first rejected this but on further pressing agreed to 'hazzard all' to please the Queen of England and to avoid her charges and the trouble of bringing in an army. On 27 March Errington again went to the Castle with this offer. When Lethington tried to buy time by requesting a copy of the Perth articles, Killigrew immediately sent them with an accompanying warning that this was their last chance for a peaceful resolution. When they returned the document with the comment that it seemed satisfactory but for one or two points which needed further elucidation, Killigrew told them bluntly that the time for prevarication was past. If they did not surrender within eight days 'they shall feel the cannon,' and if they did not directly send a written response they would never hear from him again and no further offer would be made.[19]

Errington's mission had not been completely fruitless. His observant eye was again trained on the defences. He noted that 'much labour had been expended in fortifying' the Castle since his previous visit. He estimated 'the house stronger by 10 lasts of powder and 100 men than it was then.' The Castilians were conserving their shot, apart from lobbying a few cannon balls at the new trench the Regent was constructing around the north-west side of the Castle. Grange acknowledged that he had kept back three lasts of powder pending Drury's coming which they would otherwise have expended on their adversaries. They had placed a lot of earth on the Spur outside the Castle, between the butts, to muffle the effect of cannon shot.

'They had made a rampart to cross over from one side to the other at the melting house called "the Smith's forge," and by that means had cut off all the backside of the castle that hangs towards the North West, and placed several pieces of ordnance there. They had cut off the fore part of the Spur which was before of timber and boards, and have made one high wall of lime and stone to cover them withal. They leave nothing undone that they may devise for their safeguard.'[20]

Archaeological excavations on the site of David's Tower have confirmed Errington's observations, revealing a doorway on the south side 21 feet above

51 Contemporary view of the siege of Edinburgh, 1573, showing the Castle
surrounded by 'mounts'.

the surface of the rock, well-planned for defence. Access could be gained only
by a ladder or movable steps. The hall within had recesses on either side which
could conceal defenders in an advantageous position to resist attack while a
sunken pit was probably intended as a trap just as besiegers were about to
engage the besieged.[21] These remains suggest that Grange was preparing to
fight to the very last.

   Killigrew communicated to the Regent the rules of engagement. The
English would not negotiate or come to terms with the Castilians without
consent of the Scots Privy Council, and vice versa. The English would be
under their own commander and any losses of ordnance would be made up
from that taken from the Castle, and powder and shot replaced. Those who

took part in the actual assault on the Castle would get the spoil. An exception was made for the ordnance, munitions, royal plate, jewels, wardrobe, household stuff, registers and records belonging to the King and Crown of Scotland. Grange, Lethington and Home should be taken alive to be brought before a court of law for their crimes. During the time that the English forces and ordnance were in Scotland the Scots would hand over hostages including the Regent's cousin, Argyll's bastard. Every assistance and protection was to be accorded the English force, and adequate rations provided. As a result Morton decreed that oxen were to be made ready to draw the ordnance and a cavalry detachment should provide an escort for the English army. He also urged the people of Edinburgh to give board and lodging to the occupying English forces at reasonable rates, and to fulfil their promise of providing pioneers to assist in the entrenchments.[22] Killigrew was clearly impressed by the way the Regent was preparing for the siege, and commented on how co operative he was. For instance, when the ambassador took up the cause of the wives of eight burgesses under sentence of death for their actions during the troubles, Morton spared them and banished them from the realm instead. Morton, concluded Killigrew, was doing all he could to leave no residue of bitterness. 'He has shown rigour to none since he was regent, nor executed any but one spy who was going into the Castle... [and] yet the devil is busy.'[23]

Another 'last' attempt was made by the Earl of Rothes – who stood in good repute with Grange – to bring the Castilians to terms. Twice in the first week of April Rothes visited the Castle and brought back what were brazenly called 'the demands of the Castle' as a result of his first parley. They wanted a complete amnesty, and for the lives, lands and honours of the besieged to be preserved. They also stipulated that Grange should be reimbursed his expenses and given the governorship of Blackness, and should be allowed to send the Crown Jewels to Mary who had entrusted them to him. Drury and Morton recognised the strength of their own position and were determined on unconditional surrender. These 'modest demands' being refused, Grange and Lethington declared that though deserted by all their friends, they would resist to the end.[24]

The English were now arriving in numbers and were increasingly committed to a siege. Many young bloods, including Thomas Cecil, Burghley's son, and Sir George Carey, Hunsdon's, repaired from the English court to join the army and work in the trenches. Even Killigrew lent his hand as a pioneer. On Saturday 4 April Drury ordered his gun commanders to make another assessment of the Castle. They all agreed it could not long withstand their batteries. They also surveyed the trenches which they deemed too low and too narrow. Their criticism was confirmed when, while carrying out this survey, they were shot at and very narrowly missed. The English set to work, erecting a large canopy to shield their pioneers from the view of the Castilians. Such an object was too tempting to ignore and a raiding party attempted to burn it. They managed merely to kill a tailor in his shop and a soldier, before being repulsed with loss.[25]

Finally on 20 April Sir William Drury, the Marshall of Berwick, 'sat down before the Castle.' He had with him a considerable force, although estimates varied, of between 700 and 1,500 hagbutters and pikemen. They were augmented by 500 Scots mercenaries besides the gentlemen volunteers and the citizens of Edinburgh. A few days later the ships arrived at Leith, carrying the battering train comprising a cannon royal, six double cannons, fourteen gros culverins (nine of which had been taken from the Scots at Flodden), two sakers, two Mortice pieces and two bombards or mortars. On disembarkation they were mounted on their carriages and taken to Holyrood to await the completion of the trenches and gun platforms. In addition three culverins and a demi-cannon were provided by the Regent. It was formidable force to field against the ragbag assortment that Grange had at his disposal. In addition to 160 men, including seven cannoneers, and six smiths, he was encumbered with an odd medley, including 'a bairn, a butcher, Isabel the washer, the old Norrice, Lowis a lad, and Haggye a garratour.'[26] On the other hand the Castle did have over forty cannon – including Mons Meg – with the potential to seriously hamper the besiegers' preparations. That the potential was not realised was down to shortages of both shot and powder and of cannoneers.[27]

Drury issued an ultimatum to Grange. If he surrendered the Castle and all those inside Elizabeth would intercede for their lives, but if they persisted in their opposition and obstinacy 'abiding the cannon,' then they should 'look for grace and favour' no more. A similar edict was issued in the name of King James commanding Grange, under pain of a traitor's death, to deliver the Castle and its ordnance within six hours. The Castilians still parried. They asked for the ultimatum to be put in writing, but this request was refused. They were told that the next messenger they would receive should be the cannon. The Castilians hoisted the royal standard and 'returned answer that they would keep the Castle for Queen Mary, although all Scotland and half England had sworn the contrary.'[28] Their defiance and bravado far outmatched their capacity to withstand what was to come.

And not all would withstand it. A deserter told the besieging forces that there was a real water shortage in the Castle, powder and shot were scarce, the only meat they had was salted, and that many other soldiers wanted to give up or desert. This was confirmed when a letter was found in a glove cast from the Castle asking a friend to find out if there were any hope of mercy for them and, if so, to make a prescribed sign and they would come forth. The Regent ordered that such a sign be given and also that during the night offers of mercy be shouted at the Castle along with threats for the obdurate. Nothing came of this ruse. Lord Home was blamed for quelling thoughts of dissent and mutiny. Killigrew still hoped that 'want of water' would 'drive them to cry out *"peccavi."*'[29] He gave this assessment of their chances:

> They within make good show and fortify continually to frustrate the first battery, although the Regent and others here be of opinion that they will never abide the extremity. Their water will soon be taken from them, when the ordnance shall be laid both within and without. Hope of succour is there none. And therefore their obstinacy must needs be vain.[30]

Their obstinacy was surprising and can in part be explained by the extraordinary influence which Lethington possessed and his fatal conviction that succour would come from France. His power over Grange was described by Killigrew as something like enchantment. But while Lethington, in the last stages of his illness, his nerves shattered by the continual bombardment, was fading, Grange by this time had assumed the dominant role. He was the do or die captain, and he had his own reason to resist: his sense of honour, his integrity. It was his will, not Lethington's, that buttressed those final desperate days. Although Robert Melville, John Wishart of Pitarrow, the Constable, and other leading men would have come to terms, their powder and ammunition exhausted, their food supplies and water on the point of failing, the Governor declared he would hold the Castle till he was buried in its ruins.[31] By his own words and actions he portrayed himself as the noble knight, to his last breath loyal to a lost cause.

Morton was determined that such should not be the public perception of this stubborn diehard. English guns would depose him from his rock; propaganda would knock him from his pedestal. A broadsheet was published by Robert Lekprevik, the government printer, 'that all men may better perceive how the Laird of Grange, against his faith, honour and promise, is and has been, the instrument and occasion, of the present

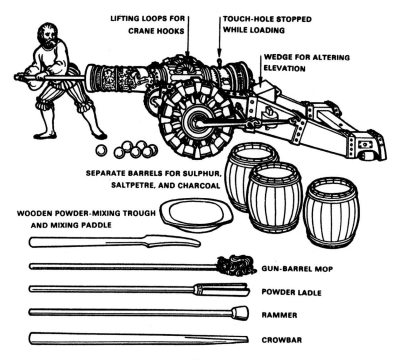

LIFTING LOOPS FOR
CRANE HOOKS

TOUCH-HOLE STOPPED
WHILE LOADING

WEDGE FOR ALTERING
ELEVATION

SEPARATE BARRELS FOR SULPHUR,
SALTPETRE, AND CHARCOAL

WOODEN POWDER-MIXING TROUGH
AND MIXING PADDLE

GUN-BARREL MOP

POWDER LADLE

RAMMER

CROWBAR

52 A cannon and its appurtenances.

unquietness and bypast vastacion of the town, to the suppressing of the exercise of God's true religion, the hindrance of justice and policy, and calamity of the whole common wealth.' It purported to be a contract between Grange and Sir Simon Preston of Craigmillar, a former Provost of Edinburgh, drawn up in the time of Moray, to defend King James against his mother's supporters who would usurp him. This was no chivalrous hero to be revered, but a vile turncoat to be extirpated.[32]

13

LIKE SNAIL IN SHELL
May 1573

A Castle strong, that neuer none assailed,
A strength that stood on mount and mighty rock,
A peerless plot, that always hath prevailed,
And above was to suffer any shock
And thought to be the only fort of fame,
Most meet and fit to bear a maiden's name...

The Scots [were] enclosed, that sat like snail in shell.
Churchyard[1]

Operations for undermining the 'Spur' or Blockhouse and erecting the batteries on the principal spots which commanded the walls proceeded with little interruption from the besieged. Fire from the Castle was desultory and hurt none but Captain Brickwell who was peppered on the face and hands with stones ricocheting from the shot, Duberie, lieutenant to Captain Strelley who was shot the first day of the siege and died of his wounds, and Nicholas Neville, a pensioner, who was wounded in the thigh. The fact that we know their names is a strong indication of the small number of casualties and the small number is attributable to scarcity of munitions in the Castle. They resisted how best they could. In mute defiance the Castilians set a Marian banner on the highest point of the Castle, David's Tower. In vocal defiance cat calls came from the Castle uttering obscenities at Elizabeth. The English took poetic revenge for the besmirching of their Queen's honour by silencing one of the 'blasphemers,' Sandy Smith, by shooting him in the throat when he came to the well.[2]

From the 'Plan of the Siege' first published in *Holinshed's Chronicles* in 1577 but taken from Johnson's contemporary sketch it is clear that the English engineers had managed to surround the Castle with terraced gun emplacements called 'mounts' upon which they placed their batteries and from which they could direct fire on all the salient points of the Castle. Behind the barricades immediately in front of the entrance to the Castle and its protecting Blockhouse they erected 'the General's two mounts,' presumably under the command of Drury himself. From this position six cannon could fire with devastating effect and at point-blank range at the Spur, the two towers and the eastern curtain wall. The only other mount named on the plan is 'the King's Mount,' commanded by Morton, which was situated due west of the Castle and alone flew the Saltire. The other four stretched from the site of the present Heriot's Hospital in the south to the northern side of the Nor Loch, and were named Mounts Drury, Sutton, Lee and Carey after their commanders, the Marshall, Sir Thomas Sutton, Sir Henry Lee and Sir George Carey. Sutton, as the most experienced cannoneer and master of ordnance in northern England, commanded the mount due south of the Castle where his guns could bear to best effect on David's Tower. Drury did not proceed piecemeal, but securely planted his ordnance as each gun emplacement was made ready. It was slow work but it was not until they were all placed that the bombardment would begin when 'they shall all speak together.'[3]

Morton was active in the siege and his efforts, and those of his soldiers were much praised by the English, who had expected less. In an effort to isolate the enemy, all former Marian soldiers and the wives of those in the Castle were prohibited from coming within four miles of Edinburgh on pain of death. Communication to and from the outside world was destined to failure. Another cipher message aimed at the castle was found when the arrow bearing it soared right over the Castle and landed in the trenches beyond. It revealed the strength of the English as 600 men, that the Marshall was lodged in Robert Gurlow's house, and that they were undermining the Blockhouse and planned to blow it up. It went on to suggest that a cannon be fired to kill the commander and his staff.[4]

On Trinity Sunday 17 May, the batteries were completed and, after church, began their own sermon by playing on the principal bastion, David's Tower. Their bombardment was met by a long and loud shriek from the women in the Castle which was distinctly heard in the English camp, 'terming the day and hour black.'[5] The soldiers within were defiant and manned the tower displaying their ensigns until they were driven from their perch by the accurate English cannon fire. Killigrew wrote:

> This day at one of the clock in the afternoon, some of our pieces began to speak such language as it made both them in the Castle, I am sure, think more of God than they did before, and all our men, and a great many others, think the enterprise not so hard as before they took it to be... Thanks be to God, although

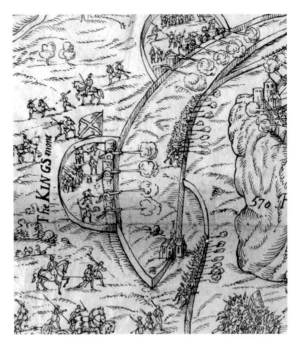

53 Detail of the siege showing 'the King's Mount' with its
Saltire cross.

it be longsome, it hath hitherto been with the least blood that ever was heard in
such a case and this conjecture we have to lead us, that they want store of
powder within, for they have suffered us to plant all the ordnances, and to shoot
yesterday all the afternoon without any harm from them.[6]

From then on the cannon played incessantly upon the Castle, provoking an
intermittent response from the guns of the garrison. On 20 May the Castilians
placed a battery behind a curtain wall around David's Tower to fire on Drury's
Mount. The following day every English battery began to deliver devastating salvos
on each side of the Castle. Mortars and bombards peppered the walls, and
demolished many of the buildings behind them. The Castilians on David's Tower
replied fiercely with about twenty-four shot, initially forcing the English gunners to
relinquish their posts until the fearless Marshall inspired them by firing the cannon
himself. All the efforts of the defenders, however, had little lasting effect other than
to expend much of their meagre resources and to redirect the English cannon from
the walls to their ordnance. The accuracy of the English gunners was impressive,
some of their shots smashing the Castle guns off their mounts. A particularly lucky
shot struck one of the largest in its mouth, shattering it, the splinters flying about

the ears of those who stood nearby. All in all the English expended some 3,000 great shot in twelve days, an impressive rate of fire for the time. Despite assurances that there was 'great husbandry of powder here,' the Queen was determined to save what she could and so the English soldiers were ordered to recover what they could. They delegated the task to the Scots who were paid a bawbee (a penny and a quarter) for every bullet they retrieved. With this inducement, the majority were found.[7]

On the afternoon of 22 May the southern wall of the great square peel, David's Tower, shattered and rent by the new explosive shells fired by Sutton's guns, collapsed, as did Constable's Tower the following day, along with the gun platform in between the two. The falling masonry sent up dense clouds of dust, burying the cannoneers and completely damning up the gate and entrance between the Castle and the outer court and Blockhouse. The old Fore Well, 16 yards north of David's Tower, was also choked by debris. Although this was the main water supply, its loss was ameliorated by the fact that its contents had long been used up. The archaeological excavation in 1912 of a structure below the level of the Half-Moon Battery (built by Morton after the siege on the site of the ruined tower) showed that on the outer face of the shot-hole the masonry was shattered, evidently the result of bombardment by cannon. The worst damage was done to the side of the tower nearest the well, and two solid iron cannon balls and fragments of burst shell were found in the debris directly beneath that wall. Outside the lines of the tower, but joined to it at the northeast corner at an angle of 110 degrees with the north face of the tower, the remains of a massive masonry wall were revealed, within which was a vaulted recess with a stone-built gun platform. In the external wall, formed by a carefully tooled ashlar, is a tapered loop-hole, oval in section and trumpet-mouthed at the interior face of the wall, its axis carefully aligned to point directly down the High Street. This is all that remains of the 'curtain with six cannons, or such like pieces in loops of stone looking in the street-ward' mentioned by Johnson and Fleming, these surviving fragments speaking eloquently of the dramatic fate that befell it.[8]

The Spur had also taken some battering and was now isolated, and at 7 a.m. on 26 May the English decided to seize it. A diversionary attack on the west side of the Castle from Lee's Mount had drawn off troops from the Spur to counter them and so resistance was much less than had been feared. The breach was large enough, and the ditch was filled up with stones and rubbish, so that the attackers could have entered there, but because it lay so open in the very mouth of the enemy's shot, it was not thought safe to make the assault at that place. As an alternative to a frontal attack ladders were provided for the troops to scale the walls of the Spur out of danger of the enemy's shot.

54 The South side of the Castle of Edinburgh, showing the vantage point from Drury's Mount.

Foremost in this service were Captain Home and the ubiquitous Captain Crawford. Home's ladder was too short and when one of his men was shot off behind him he was forced to come down again. Crawford with his experience of scaling castle walls took charge and soon clambered up, followed by Home and the rest of the soldiers without further loss. They found that the garrison had fled the Spur and had been hoisted into the Castle. The only resistance came from some harquebus shot from the Castle walls, for the heavy ordnance were too high above them to be able to direct fire upon them. The relieved men rushed forward and planted a *corps de garde* before the gate of the Blockhouse, called Hume's Porter-Lodge. The operation was completed and the ensign of the general raised at 10 a.m. The English lost eight men in the diversion and twenty were hurt or slain in the taking of the Spur.[9] The fall of the Spur also entailed the loss of another well which had furnished a pint of water per man per day.

Of those remaining in the Castle, many were hurt, all were hungry and thirsty, and some were suffering from water poisoning. The garrison was both too small for the defence and too large to be sustained by the remaining food and water. There were mutterings among the soldiery exacerbated by the niggardly provisions and the rationing undertaken by Grange's wife, a compensation given her by her husband to overlook his dalliance with her maid. Some fled over the walls unhindered by Grange. 'Let them go,' said Grange, 'our provisions are scant and the house is better without them.' But with the remainder on the verge of mutiny Grange conceded that further resistance was futile. The immovable object had been rendered by the irresistible force as a rock eventually yields to the sea.

On 27 May a ship loaded with powder arrived in Leith, and preparations were being laid for a general assault, when at 5 p.m., after the beating of a drum, Grange appeared on the Castle wall and descended by rope with a white rod in his hand. He asked for a cessation of hostilities in order for talks with his English counterparts preparatory to surrender. This granted, a two-hour evening meeting took place in the Lawnmarket between Grange and Robert Melville on the one hand, and Killigrew and Drury on the other. The uninvited Regent insisted on sending Lord Boyd as his representative to the meeting. Grange asked that he be allowed to retire to his own lands in Fife, that Home and Lethington be allowed to go to England, and that lives of all the others be spared and their properties respected. To these conditions the Marshall would probably have agreed, but Drury could go no further in acceding to these requests than the Regent and the ambassador would allow.[10] When Morton heard of them he was adamantly opposed. He replied with an

55 Detail of the Siege, showing the Spur and the fire power unleashed against it.

56 Detail of the siege, showing the Castle under siege from all sides.
David's Tower is the most prominent and central feature.

ultimatum expiring at 9 p.m. He would let the majority of the garrison live if they came out singly, carrying only their own baggage, and submitted to his mercy. Eleven were exempt from this pardon: Grange, Lethington, John Maitland, Home, Robert Melville, Dunkeld, Logan of Restalrig, Crichton of Drylaw, Pitarrow, and the coiners James Mossman and James Cockie. These individuals were required to submit unconditionally. Their fates would be determined by Elizabeth in accordance with the treaty made between that monarch and James VI.[11]

Recognising that their lives were forfeit they rejected these terms and declared their resolution to resist. Their soldiers, however, were no longer prepared to sacrifice their own lives in a hopeless cause. They threatened to hang Lethington over the walls within six hours if he did not advise surrender, and were ready to deliver Grange and his companions to Morton. In this dilemma an expedient was adopted which might preserve their pride if not their lives. Grange sent secretly to Drury, in consequence of which two English companies led by Drury himself were admitted within the walls on the evening of 28 May. To them – not to the Scots – Grange and his men surrendered. The poor remnant of the Castle marched out in armour, with their swords belted on, and banner flying. A strong guard of the Regent's troops escorted them as a protection from the ire of the citizenry. In addition to their leaders, the survivors numbered some 164 men, thirty-four women, and ten boys. Grange, Lethington and the other senior men were taken to Drury's quarters with their arms still on them and received with courtesy.[12]

The Castle sprouted the ensign of the English general, and many an English soldier clambered into it by the great hole in the east curtain so that they could boast on their return home that they had breached the hitherto inviolate 'Maiden.' Once the Castle was handed over to the Regent's bastard half-brother, Sir George Douglas of Parkhead, however, and its ruined walls came under the command of Captains Home and Crawford, the English were no longer allowed inside in great numbers, but were bluntly repelled with the thrust pike and the levelled harquebus.[13]

Once secured the Castle was searched. Not much was found. The English suspected that Lethington had ordered all incriminating papers relating to their association with the French and Spanish to be burned. Those that survived revealed the ironic but unsurprising news that France was determined to aid them and Spain was non-committal.[14] In Grange's rooms were found not just papers, but the crown, sword and sceptre broken and hidden in a wooden chest along with an inventory of royal jewels pawned or given to supporters who had financed the Castilians in return. Morton made it his immediate business to retrieve the lot, even sending Lady Lennox to get Drury to return a ring that Grange had given him.[15] None of the English guns were damaged in the action, but a lot of powder and shot had been expended. The capture of the Castle yielded far less of either than Elizabeth had anticipated. She was to get little recompense for her pains and expense other than the satisfaction of a successful conclusion to an unnecessary civil war and siege.

The High Kirk of St Giles, for so long a military outpost, reverted to its ecclesiastical role by holding a service of thanksgiving for the end of the troubles, triumphalism tinged with demands for revenge.

14

A JUST RECOMPENSE
June and July 1573

They have not spared the sons of God, the people being there convened
in time of divine service, thinking in that place to be shot of ordnance to
have murdered the greater multitude, and by discharging of their
ordnance against women, children and impotent persons, whose slaughter
on the streets has been their greatest victory, as also by fire raising in the
town, which they thought utterly to have destroyed so soon as they
found the wind favourable to the execution of their precogitat mischief,
liberally spending their shot where any appearance was to quench the
flame, so that they doubt not their cruelties have been brought home to
them, and their doings to be detested of all the godly and honest who,
they hope, shall not find them worthy of mercy and favour that
heretofore being offered they rejected, but will allow that they be
recompensed with such punishment as they justly deserved.

The Regent Morton[1]

In Leith, supervising the loading of the ordnance, powder, bullets and other
munitions onto the ships which would return them safely to England, Drury
anxiously waited his next orders. Grange and Lethington were lodged with
him in his quarters in Gourlay's house, a fine old edifice on the Old Bank
Close. Lethington should have stayed with Killigrew but the clamour of the
people was such that Drury had to take charge of them for their own safety.
The common people jeered and threw stones as they passed along after the
surrender. Raucous sermons of the ministers added to the lynch-mob
atmosphere.[2] They were safer with him than anywhere else in Edinburgh. For
three days the senior prisoners remained largely at liberty and Robert Melville
stayed with his brother James in the latter's house. Then before dawn on 3 June
they were taken to Leith and put in ward to await their fate.

57 Reconstruction of the Castle after 1573. The Half-Moon Battery is being built around the remains of David's Tower.

Humbled, Lethington and Grange wasted no time in trying to get English protection, writing in a desperate staccato to the Queen's chief minister Burghley and to Leicester, her favourite. 'The malice of our enemies is the more increased against us... we doubt not that they will crave our blood at her Majesty's hands.' They begged not to be turned over to the vengeful spirits of their fellow countrymen. They offered faithful future service to Elizabeth and, recalling old friendship with Burghley, asked him to intercede for them: 'There was never time wherein your lordship's friendship might stand us in such stead. As we have oftentimes heretofore tasted thereof, so we humbly pray you let it

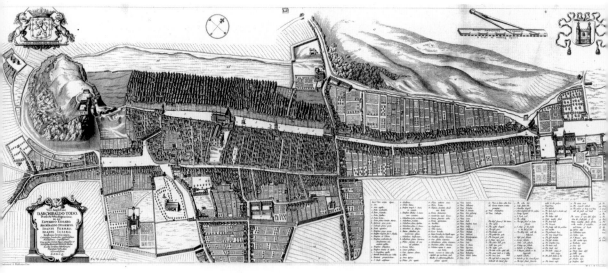

58 Bird's eye view of the rebuilt Castle in 1647.

not inlack us now, in time of this our great misery, when we have more need that ever we had.' Burghley was dubious about their sincerity and disinclined to intervene. Lethington could conduct his own defence without his help, and he would leave him to it.[3]

If Lethington was left to be the inadequate advocate in his own cause, Morton, as chief counsel for the prosecution, was better able to influence the English tribunal. He wrote to Burghley entreating an immediate decision on the prisoners' fate and imploring that they be handed over to him to pay for their crimes.[4] Killigrew also advised that they be executed, thinking them now 'fitter for God than for the world.' Good news for the prisoners would be 'ill news to the most and best part of Scotland.' Elizabeth, as usual, did not act in haste but requested information to be sent to her of the 'quality and quantity of the prisoners' offences.' With the intention of whipping up Elizabeth's greatest fears of a Spanish invasion, Killigrew dispatched to London incriminating documents found in the Castle including a letter sent by Alva. He told Burghley that 'the unthankfullest thing that may come out of England to the Regent and the best Scots here will be any suit in favour of the three chief prisoners, or any suspending of their execution.' By such lenity Elizabeth could forfeit all the goodwill she had gained by the 'expugnation' of the Castle. Killigrew and Morton united so determinedly that she eventually acquiesced and ordered that the prisoners be handed over to the Regent to be dealt with as he pleased. Killigrew was to instruct the Regent to keep them in some safe place and out of reach of their mortal enemies where they may be in fear of being murdered, there to remain until the charges had been put and their answer made. As soon as that was done 'we may further understand the particularity of each man's crime.' The Queen also wrote to Morton more or less abdicating to him the decision as to what to do with the prisoners.[5] She was signing their death warrant, at least for some. For Robert Melville she did successfully intercede. Drury was sent instructions to relinquish his prisoners and to return home, but not before ensuring that her ordnance and as many soldiers as possible were sent back 'for easing of our charges.' She need not have worried, they had been dispatched before her letter got to its recipient.

Lethington, infirm, wretched and despondent, escaped Morton's clutches by dying in the Leith Tolbooth – still in Drury's custody – on 9 June, most probably of his ailments.[6] He had been the intellectual backbone of the resistance and it was round him that the Marian nobility had marshalled. But his personal influence had waned when he was cut off from the outside world. Left to their own devices these magnificent lords had one by one caved in. Abandoned by his betters, the old Secretary, now past his prime, had stubbornly clung on to a phantasmal hope of foreign rescue. His disdain for the Jacobean nobility ranged against him and his determination not to yield to their ultimata were expressions more of pride than of policy. At the last his complex and subtle mind had ossified into a singularity of obdurate defiance since he could not bare to see his ambitions turn to dust and his career end in utter failure. Death came as a mercy, sparing him the rope and further humiliation. His spirit had flown but the husk remained. His redoubtable wife, Mary Fleming, loyal to the last and to his memory, by a moving personal plea to Burghley, saved his wasted corpse from the humiliation of the state treason trial that had befallen the fourth Earl of Huntly. In a firm letter to Morton, Elizabeth pointed out that such barbarous habits were extremely distasteful to the English sensibility: 'It is not our manner in this country to show cruelty upon the dead bodies so unconvicted, but to suffer them straight to be buried and put in the earth.' (The English, of course, reserved their cruelties for the living.) As God had allowed him to die of natural causes so the Regent should allow him to be buried naturally and not 'pulled in pieces.' The Marshall was petitioned by Athol and others for a decent burial. He tried his best to persuade the Regent, but in vain, and Calderwood states that so long did the decaying corpse remain unburied that the vermin from it came creeping out under the door of the house where he was.[7] When or where one of the most significant personages of his age was finally buried is not known, although the family vault at Haddington is the best bet.

On 16 June Drury reluctantly complied with the orders from his Queen, handed over Grange and the rest into the hands of the Regent, and, his task completed, marched his remaining troops back to Berwick. The prisoners were split up, the lesser being dispersed to secure prisons outside Edinburgh. Home, however, was committed to the Castle he had so lately relinquished. James Kirkcaldy and the two 'coiners' were held in the Tolbooth. Grange was kept separately in the gloomy recesses of Holyrood under Morton's watchful eye. His prey would not escape.

While in Holyrood Grange refused to give up hope, and penned a love letter to the girl who had borne him a child. Even it was seized and deciphered. The old soldier still had some loyal friends and relations, and 100 of them offered to put themselves under bonds of manrent to the house of Angus and Morton and to pay the Regent £20,000 with an annuity of 300 merks in return for his life. If Morton were tempted the 'denunciations of the preachers' steadied him. They cried out that 'God's plague would not cease till the land were purged with blood.' The success of Drury had fulfilled the first part of Knox's death bed prophecy that Grange should be shamefully dragged from the rock wherein he trusted. As Tytler remarks, the vehemence with which the clergy 'opposed every intercession for mercy, affords a melancholy proof of their determination that the second head of the reputed prophecy should be punctually accomplished.'[8] But Morton, no matter how venal he was, was not tempted to mercy. He was determined 'to bring down that giant's pride who, as they alleged, presumed to be another Wallace.'

His end was ignominious. On Monday 3 August 1573 Grange, his brother James, and the two coiners were put on trial for murder and treason, and were convicted. They were straightaway put into a cart and drawn slowly backwards from Holyrood Abbey to the Mercat Cross in the High Street of Edinburgh. There they were to be hanged in the presence of an immense crowd of onlookers. They were attended on the scaffold by Mr David Lindsay, an old friend of Grange, and a martial clergyman, in whose hands, if we may believe Melville, it was difficult to say whether the Bible or the hagbut was the more congenial instrument. Melville got it from Lindsay himself that Grange received his ministrations with gratitude, asked him to repeat Knox's last words concerning him, and expressed on the scaffold both deep penitence for his sins and an unshaken attachment to his captive sovereign. His final words to Lindsay were, 'I hope in God, that after men shall think me past and gone, I shall give you a token of the assurance of that mercy to my soul, according to the speech of that man of God.' At about 4 p.m. when the sun was shining from the north-west corner of the steeple, he was thrust off the scaffold.[9] For a while he hung there facing east, but gradually the body swung on the rope towards the west and remained facing the sun. Lindsay recalled that when he seemed to be dead he lifted up his hands, which were bound before him, and laid them down again softly. In his death he paid tribute to the great prophet whose friendship he had spurned and whose holy cause he had betrayed. Well perhaps, or was the execution carried out thus in order to verify that prophecy? His brother James and the 'counterfeiters,' James Mossman and James Cockie, were executed with him, like the thieves accompanying Christ. After being suspended for some time on the gibbet, their bodies were quartered, and their heads were cut off and spiked on the most conspicuous parts of the Castle walls, Grange's most prominently on the ruined entrance gate. That night Knox's successor as minister of St Giles led his congregation in giving thanks to God's mercy and Queen Elizabeth's guns for their deliverance.[10]

The other state prisoners were allowed to live. Dunkeld was incarcerated in Blackness, Robert Melville was banished for a year to Lethington and Lethington's younger brother John was sent to Tantallon. Lord Home was spared as a result of the intercession of his kinsmen, the lairds of Manderston and Coldenknowes, but was not released from the Castle until shortly before his death in 1575.[11] The disbanded garrison who had been thrust into the dungeons of Merchiston, Blackness and Craigmillar were soon all allowed to depart with bag and baggage as promised. More punitive measures were unnecessary.

Reprisals were restrained and largely confined to fines. On 31 July the large-scale trial of burgesses began. Those in the town who had remained there during its occupation were called to account and had to 'compone for their lyff.' They were fined with varying degrees of severity, dropping dramatically as time went on. For instance John Hart of the Canongate 'for supplying victuals and other necessaries' to the rebels, was fined £66 13s 4d; John Short for the same crime £20; and David Scorguy and Robert Davidson £10 and £6 13s 4d respectively.[12] Most came from the lowest reaches of society, but occasionally a prominent figure appeared. On one occasion the session had to decide if Thomas MacCalzean of Cliftonhall, a senator of the College of Justice, should be forced to appear barefoot and in sackcloth to confess his fault at the pillar of St Giles. On another the session was highly embarrassed when Adam Fullerton himself was accused by the Fairlie family of peculation. He was a canny man of business and politics and may well have been a war profiteer. The accusations were, of course, summarily dismissed.

Thus only a few executions and not many fines marked the end of a bloody and bitter civil war. By a policy towards the defeated of reconciliation Morton brought peace and harmony to the war-ravaged kingdom, and it was not mere official puff to say that his regency 'pacified the seditions and civil war by which the realm was miserably afflicted, wherethrough our sovereign's lieges enjoyed a reasonable quietness and rest during the time of his regiment.'[13]

Morton left a further indelible mark on the landscape by his repair and expansion of the Castle's defences. The Spur was rebuilt more or less as it had been. Around the ruins of David's Tower he erected the present Half-Moon Battery with its deep-mouthed embrasures and massive front. The Portcullis Gate was built on the site of Constable's Tower, and over it, above the royal arms, he caused his own coat of arms – the heart of Douglas with three mullets, quartered with the bearings of Dalkeith and Lochleven – to be placed. Ultimately his hubris was to be his downfall. Soon after James VI came into his personal rule the young King arrested and beheaded the former Regent, ostensibly for his alleged involvement in the murder of Darnley, but in reality because he posed a threat to the position of the royal favourites. His corpse was buried in an insignificant plot in Greyfriar's churchyard, while his head was spiked more prominently on the Tolbooth.

At the same time the King ordered Grange's remains, which by another irony were probably buried in Greyfriar's, to be re-interred honourably in the ancient burial place of his predecessors in Kinghorn, a singular recognition by James of

59 The stark and simple burial place of the Regent Morton in Greyfriar's churchyard.

the merit of his mother's champion.[14] As a mark of his total rehabilitation in the eyes of posterity, on the entrance to the same gate upon which Morton's arms were displayed now stands a twentieth-century plaque to his old adversary, the erstwhile Captain of the Castle, William Kirkcaldy of Grange, a romantic reminder of a dying cause. But is it deserved? Whatever the virtues of Grange's long championship of his Queen, his obduracy towards the end, his bitter resistance when all hope had faded, like that of his mentor Lethington, had merely prolonged the pointless agony of the long-suffering population of the town as well as of the garrison of the Castle. Grange is guilty of many unnecessary deaths and much futile destruction. His integrity and steely defiance came at a price, a price paid for a long time by others. Ultimately he, too, paid the price, and time has forgiven. With his death the reign of Mary Queen of Scots properly ends. Her champions were no more than legends. Resistance to the Jacobean cause was over.

60 Maitland of Lethington, in younger and happier days.

CONCLUSION

The victory of the King's party was never inevitable and was due to many factors. Mary's precipitate flight to England meant that the icon for which they were struggling was beyond her supporters' reach. The longer she remained in exile, the less hope there was of her return and the more her cause became quixotic. The spectacular fall of Dumbarton and the botched raid on Stirling with the attendant death of an unpopular Regent further hastened the end. The Massacre of St Bartholomew's Day fatally compromised those who looked to France for succour. But most significant were two linked factors.

In the last resort, Charles IX of France, bedevilled with internecine conflict between Catholic and Huguenot at home, for all his half-promises of aid and armies, sent little of the former and none of the latter. Nor did Spanish help materialise, since Spain was immersed in protracted campaigns in the Netherlands, and was always uneasy about French ambitions. The rivalry and distrust between the two great Catholic powers prevented any united effort to intervene on Mary's behalf. Elizabeth of England, penny-pinching, prevaricating constantly, promising nothing and forever urging the Scots to settle their own differences by their own resources, ultimately intervened decisively. She would not, in the last analysis, allow her great rival's forces to triumph. She kept Mary under lock and key, and at critical moments in the years of civil war she reluctantly dispatched English soldiers, English generals, and, most significantly, English artillery to buttress the party of the little King and reduce the great 'Maiden Castle' to submission. Foreign intervention in the otherwise evenly-matched Scottish Civil War tipped the balance and did so conclusively since in the end only one foreign power intervened. England, as ever, proved decisive in Scottish affairs.

The Scottish Civil War cannot claim the significance of the later Civil War in England. The shape of the constitution and the role of monarchy within the nation did not depend on its outcome. James VI would have come to the throne in time in any case and probably as early as he did. Had the Marians vanquished their opponents, they would have still been without a Queen since Elizabeth was unlikely to return her great rival. Royal lieutenants would have ruled in her stead, headed by a Hamilton no doubt, or perhaps by a Huntly, but with a privy council which would have included many prominent members of the King's party. Neither Lethington nor Grange was the spearhead of a Catholic revival, nor did they espouse a view of kingship very different from that of the King's party or of the King. Their actions sprang from personal loyalty to Mary, who for all her faults – and neither of her champions were blind to them – was in their eyes still the legitimate monarch to whom they had pledged allegiance.

Thus this was a civil war upon which little hinged in the long term, making the sufferings inflicted by and upon both sides and on many in between all the more pointless. That is a factor we should bare in mind when we assess what could be seen as a chivalrous and noble defiance on the part of Edinburgh and its Castle.

CHRONOLOGY

GLOSSARY

NOTES

BIBLIOGRAPHY

LIST OF ILLUSTRATIONS

BIOGRAPHICAL INDEX

INDEX OF PLACES

GENERAL INDEX

CHRONOLOGY

1561
19 AUGUST: Mary Queen of Scots landed in Scotland.

1565
29 JULY: Mary married Darnley.

1566
9 MARCH: Murder of Ricchio.
19 JUNE: James VI born.

1567
9-10 FEBRUARY: Murder of Darnley.
15 JUNE: Battle of Carberry Hill.
24 JULY: Mary abdicated.
29 JULY: James VI crowned.
10 AUGUST: Kirkcaldy commissioned to pursue Bothwell.
22 AUGUST: Moray proclaimed Regent.
1 SEPTEMBER: Balfour surrendered Edinburgh Castle to Moray.
5 SEPTEMBER: Kirkcaldy made Governor of Edinburgh Castle and Provost of Edinburgh.
1 OCTOBER: Surrender of Dunbar Castle.

1568
2 MAY: Mary escaped from Lochleven Castle.
13 MAY: Battle of Langside.
26 NOVEMBER: Moray denounced Mary at Westminster Conference.

1569
3 SEPTEMBER: Arrest of Lethington and Balfour.
NOVEMBER: Northern Rising to free Mary Queen of Scots.
20 DECEMBER: Northern Rising collapsed.

1570
23 JANUARY: Moray assassinated.
14 FEBRUARY: Moray buried in St Giles Kirk; Lethington acquitted by the Privy Council.
17 JULY: Lennox appointed Regent.

1571

27 JANUARY: Lennox leaves Edinburgh.

MARCH: Counterfeit skirmish.

2 APRIL: Dumbarton Castle captured.

29 APRIL: Netherbow Port skirmish, beginnng of 'the wars between Leith and Edinburgh.'

13-20 MAY: The First Siege of Edinburgh

2 JUNE: Edmonston Edge skirmish.

16 JUNE: Drury's Peace or Black Saturday.

13 JULY: Holyrood skirmish.

22 AUGUST: Netherbow skirmish.

28 AUGUST: Stirling Parliament.

4 SEPTEMBER: Stirling Raid. Lennox assassinated.

5 SEPTEMBER: Mar appointed Regent.

16-21 OCTOBER: Second Siege of Edinburgh.

17 OCTOBER: Battle of Tulliangus.

20 NOVEMBER: Battle of Crabstone.

NOVEMBER: Discovery of the Ridolphi plot to replace Elizabeth with Mary.

10 DECEMBER: Boroughmuir skirmish.

1572

MARCH: Boroughmuir skirmish.

27 MARCH: Treaty of Blois.

6 APRIL: Jedburgh skirmish.

MAY: Cragingate Skirmish.

28 MAY: Northumberland surrendered to the English.

3 JUNE: Cragingate skirmish.

10 JUNE: Cragingate skirmish.

30 JUNE: Holyrood skirmish.

6 JULY: Battle of Brechin.

24 AUGUST: St Bartholomew's Day Massacre.

28 OCTOBER: Mar died.

24 NOVEMBER: Knox died: Morton appointed Regent.

1573

4 FEBRUARY: skirmish in Trenches.

7 FEBRUARY: skirmish at St Giles.

12 FEBRUARY: Fire raising in Edinburgh.

23 FEBRUARY: Pacification of Perth.

16-28 MAY: Third Siege of Edinburgh Castle.

28 MAY: Surrender of Edinburgh Castle.

9 JUNE: Lethington dies.

3 AUGUST: Grange executed.

GLOSSARY OF ORDNANCE

BASILISK
Large siege cannon, usually made of brass, often of great length, firing 200-pound balls. Named after the fabulous reptile born of a serpent from a cock's egg (also called a cockatrice) whose breath was fatal.

BASTION
The strong-point of an artillery fortification, with two faces meeting at an angle and two flanks which join the faces to the curtain walls.

BOMBARD
An early form of a very large cannon. The term applies to both the forged iron engines, and the stone-shot discharged from them. The Great Bombards were the biggest artillery pieces, and included such as the six ton, 13 foot, $19\frac{1}{2}$inch calibre Mons Meg of 1447. They were the chief battering guns. Cumbersome, slow to load with a minimal rate of fire, they had a limited breaking strain and so gave low-impact velocity. Mons Meg could fire 350-pound gun stones a distance of two miles. It could, however, fire only about eight a day.

BLOCKHOUSE OR BULWARK
Used loosely for a strong-point, generally of earth or masonry, and specifically of an Italianate angle bastion, placed in front a fortress. It was designed exclusively for gun-powdered artillery.

CALIVER
A light kind of musket or harquebus introduced in the sixteenth century, so light that it required no rest.

CANNON
Once a generic term for artillery, but from 1500 used in the specific sense of the largest of the cast bronze guns, used as a battering piece. A double cannon, great cannon or cannon royal had a bore of about 7 inches. It could fire 50-pound iron shot over 2,000 yards. The demi-cannon was the second largest of the 'standard' range of guns, with a 6-inch bore, firing shot of up to 40 pounds over 1,700 yards. These guns could be fired about sixty or seventy times a day with a crew of two gunners and ten assistants. They were greedy of powder.

CANNON BALL

Or gun stone, as it was properly called in early days, was at first stone or granite, far cheaper but far less effective than iron. By the middle of the sixteenth century the great proportion of cannon balls were made of iron.

CORNPOWDER: SEE GUN POWDER

CULVERIN

Meaning 'snake.' A medium-heavy long-range cast bronze gun, used as the normal field gun, and on ships. With their long range and accuracy they were ideal for parapet mounting where they could discomfit the besieger's men and artillery. The gros or great culverin was the largest with a length of 10-15 feet, and bore of $5-5\frac{1}{2}$ inches, and could fire a 17-pound iron ball 2,500 yards. The demi-culverin had a bore $4\frac{1}{2}$ inches and fired shot of 8-12 pounds. Culverins Pikemoyen, and Culverins Moyen were smaller.

CURTOW

Used in England but not Scotland to describe cannon, but were originally larger than cannon. Used as a battering piece.

CUT-THROAT

A Scottish term for small artillery piece, 4-feet long with a 2-inch bore.

FALCON

The fifth in size of the guns of the culverin type. Long, slender, carriage-mounted bronze field guns firing $2\frac{1}{2}$-3 pound shot. For use against soldiers and sometimes used in fortresses. The double Falcon had a bore of about $2\frac{1}{2}$ inches, the quarter falcon about $1\frac{1}{2}$ inches.

FALCONET

Sixth in size of the guns of the culverin type, firing $1\frac{1}{2}$-pound shot. A gun of this size could be fired 140 times a day with only a small crew.

GUN POWDER

Gun powder was ground fine or 'mealed', but later it was coarse or 'corned.' Much was imported into England and Scotland from the Continent, and as England's isolation grew so her sources of supply dried up and had to be replaced by smuggling and the setting up of powder mills.

HARQUEBUS

An early type of portable trigger-operated firearm, weighing about 10-pounds and firing a half-ounce lead ball, fired resting on a tripod. The English term was hackbut or arquebus.

HAGBUTS OF CROC

Or hackbuts, the smallest fortress and field artillery pieces, with hooks on the underside of their barrels for mounting purposes instead of trunnions. They were mounted on trestles in forts and on carts in the field.

LAST
2,400 pounds A single last of powder would serve about 2,000 harquebusiers for one day.

LIZARD
An English term, possibly for a lesser culverin firing 12-pound shot.

MINION
Small kind of ordnance with a $3\frac{1}{2}$-inch bore firing 4-pound shot.

MOUNTAINS
Bulwarks.

MORTAR
Invented in the fourteenth century, the earliest of European firearms. A short piece of ordnance with a large bore and small chamber for throwing shells at high angles.

MUSKET
Named after the Italian for 'sparrow hawk', it was heavier than the caliver, had a longer barrel and fired a heavier ball over a greater distance which could pierce all but the thickest armour. Introduced into England by the 1560s.

POT-GUN: SEE MORTAR.

SAKER
An English term for a species of old cannon smaller than a demi-culverin and bigger than a minion, with a bore of about third of an inch, firing a 5-pound shot. Used on ships and in sieges.

SERPENTINE
A long-barrelled artillery piece, with a $2\frac{1}{2}$ to $3\frac{1}{2}$-inch calibre, firing 5-pound iron shot, used in sieges and on ships. Often breech loading.

SLANGS OR SLINGS
From the German Schlange meaning serpent, a term sometimes used for Serpentines, but sometimes for a heavy piece of up to 18 feet long and $\frac{3}{4}$-inch bore. Used as a battering piece.

NOTES

ABBREVIATIONS

CBP   *Calendar of Border Papers.*
CSP(F)   *Calendar of State Papers Relating to Foreign Affairs.*
CSP(S)   *Calendar of State Papers Relating to Scottish Affairs.*
RPC(S)   *Register of the Privy Council of Scotland.*
RPS(S)   *Register of the Privy Seal of Scotland* (*Registrum Magni Sigilli Regum
           Scotorum*).
J&S   'Journal of the siege' and 'Survey of the castle and town', both 1573, in
           The Bannatyne Miscellany, 1836, ii, pp.65–80.

All other citations give merely the surname of the author and/or the first word[s] of the
title. The full citation may be found in the bibliography.

INTRODUCTION

1. Quoted from Oldbuck, ch. iv, cited in *Satirical Poems*, p.182.
2. Bannatyne, p.38.
3. Mathieson, *Politics*, pp.118f; Lee, *Maitland*, p.24.
4. Knox, *History*, ii, pp.106-134.

Chapter 1
HURTLING TOWARDS DISASTER

1. *Satirical Poems*, p.70.
2. For a detailed account of the life and death of this imperious Earl see my *Blood Feud:
   The Stewarts and Gordons at War*, Tempus, 2002.
3. CSP(S), ii, p.325ff (Kirkcaldy to Bedford, 26 April and 8 May 1567).
4. CSP(S), ii, p.378 (Kirkcaldy to Bedford, 10 August 1567).
5. MacIvor, pp.144f.

6. List made by Sir James Balfour of the cannon in Edinburgh Castle, 20 March 1566, printed in Grant's, *Memoirs*, pp.368f; MacIvor, pp.60f; Goodare, p.145, note 41.
7. Morrison, p.273.
8. Lynch, *Edinburgh*, p.9.
9. Lynch, *Edinburgh*, pp.2-3.

Chapter 2
THE DEVIL'S EGG

1. *Satirical Poems*, p.112.
2. CSP(S), ii, p.373 (Throckmorton to Elizabeth, 9 August 1567).
3. CSP(S), ii, p.388 (Throckmorton to Cecil, 23 August 1567).
4. CSP(S), ii, p.397 (Moray to Cecil, 14 October 1567).
5. CSP(S), ii, p.472 (News out of Scotland, 1 August 1568).
6. CSP(S), ii, p.488 (Argyll, Huntly etc to Elizabeth, 24 August 1568).
7. CSP(S), ii, p.594 (Kirkcaldy to the Regent, 31 December 1568).
8. Melville, p.219; *Historie*, pp.39f; Grant, *Memorials*, p.105.
9. CSP(S), ii, p.658 (Moray to Elizabeth, 7 July 1569).
10. CSP(S), ii, pp.666f. (Hunsdon to Cecil, 5 August 1569); Calderwood, ii, 490.
11. Warrender, p.63 & 66 (Lethington to Norfolk, 16 September 1569).
12. Spottiswoode, ii, p.118; Melville, p.219; Herries, p.118.
13. *Diurnal*, p.152; Calderwood, iii, p.507; Tytler, p.54.
14. CSP(S), ii, p.516 (Offence by the Queen's party, 4 October 1568); *Diurnal*, p.153; Dennison, p.21.
15. CSP(F) 1569-71, p.155 (Instructions for George Carey, 22 December 1569); p.157 (Hunsdon to the Queen, 30 December 1569); CSP(S), iii, p.45 (Allen King to Sir Henry Percy, 6 January 1570). Lee, *Moray*, pp.270f.
16. CSP(F) 1569-71, p.173 (Hunsdon to Cecil, 24 January 1570); p.183 (Drury to Cecil, 7 February 1570); *Diurnal*, p.156.

Chapter 3
THE SOUL OF ALL THE GODLESS BAND

1. Maxwell, p.121.
2. CSP(F) 1569-71, p.313 (Elizabeth to Sussex, 11 August 1570).
3. CSP(F) 1569-71, p.227 (Sussex to Elizabeth, 23 April 1570).
4. Warrender, p.81; Hume, pp.311f. A Commendator is a layman receiving the revenues of an abbey, priory, monastery or other benefice.
5. Tytler, p.62; Grant, *Memorials*, p.107.
6. He so signed himself in a letter to Cecil of 2 January 1570: CSP(F) 1569-71, p.164.
7. *Diurnal*, p.158; Tytler, p.61
8. CSP(S), iii, p.92 (Randolph to Cecil, 1 March 1570); Melville, p.224.
9. CSP(F) 1569-71, p.206 (Hunsdon to Cecil, 17 March 1570); Bannatyne, p.52; Buchanan, pp.xci-ci; Calderwood, pp.554f; Lee, *Maitland*, p.32.
10. CSP(S), iii, p.127 (John Gordon to Elizabeth, 18 April 1570).
11. CSP(S), iii, 145f (Sussex to Elizabeth, 1 May 1570).

12. CSP(F) 1569-71, p.231 (Grange to Randolph, 26 April 1570); CSP(S), iii, pp.147f. (Randolph to Grange & Cecil, 1 and 2 May 1570).

13. CSP(S), iii, p.155f (Sussex to Grange and Maitland, 4 May 1570); p.180 (Maitland to Cecil, 17 May 1570); Bannatyne, p.39.

14. CSP(S), iii, p.178 (Sussex to Elizabeth, 17 May 1570); p.180 (Sussex to Cecil, 17 May 1570); Warrender, p.91.

15. CSP(F) 1569-71, p.248 (Sussex to Grange and Lethington, 14 May 1570).

16. CSP(S), iii, pp.198 (Expeditions into Scotland, 1 June 1570). *Diurnal*, p.174.

17. CSP(S), iii, p.178 (Lennox to Cecil, 17 May 1570); p.192 (Morton to the Commendator of Dunfermline, 30 May 1570); Holinshed, v, pp.646f; *Diurnal*, p.177.

18. CSP(S), iii, p.184 (Lennox to Sussex, 18 May 1570); pp.199f. (Moon to Randolph, and Sussex to Elizabeth 2 June 1570).

19. Bannatyne, p.43; Calderwood, p.560; CSP(S), iii, p.203 (Randolph to Sussex, 9 June 1570).

20. CSP(F) 1569-71, p.264, 273 (Charles IX to the French Ambassador and to Elisabeth, 10 and 19 June 1570); p.281 (Accounts of the Army in the North, 29 June 1570); Holinshed, v, p.647.

21. CSP(S), iii, p.292 (Sussex to Cecil, 6 August 1570).

22. CSP(S), iii, pp.266ff, 271f. (Election to Regent and Sussex to Cecil, 17 and 19 July 1570), p.280 (Maitland to Huntly, 24 July 1570); Hume p.314.

23. CSP(S), iii, pp.228ff. (Maitland to Sussex, and Sussex to Cecil, 18 and 24 June 1570); pp.285f. (Randolph to Sussex, and M. De Poigny's Credit 31 July 1570); p.297 (Sussex to Maitland, 7 August 1570); CSP(F) 1569-71, p.293 (Sussex to Cecil, 13 July 1570); Warrender, pp.92f.

24. CSP(S), iii, p.316 (Randolph to Sussex, 14 August 1570); *Diurnal*, p.183. Holinshed, v, p.648; Hume, p.315.

25. CSP(S), iii, pp.318f. (Randolph to Sussex, 17 August 1570); *Diurnal*, pp.186, 199; *Historie*, p.64; Bannatyne, pp.53-60; Calderwood, iii, p.10.

26. *Diurnal*, p.192.

27. Melville, pp.233f.

28. Bannatyne, p.70f; *Diurnal*, p.197; Calderwood, iii, pp.20-23; Lynch, *Edinburgh*, p.129.

29. Bannatyne, p.72; Kerr, pp.90f.

30. Calderwood, iii, p.24.

31. CSP(F) 1569-71, p.417 (Drury to Burghley, 11 March 1571); Bannatyne, pp.80-82, 91-103; *Diurnal*, p.201; Calderwood, iii, p.29

32. Bannatyne, p.91.

Chapter 4
DUMBARTON ROCK

1. Bannatyne, p.53.

2. *Diurnal*, p.205; *Historie*, p.72; Bannatyne, p.104.

3. Warrender, p.84.

4. Bannatyne, p.53; Calderwood, iii, pp.12, 55.

5. Written for Knox and preserved along with account to the Regent in Bannatyne, pp.104-7. Other accounts are to be found in *Diurnal*, p.203; Buchanan, xx, pp.28-32; *Historie*, pp.70f; Holinshed, v, p.649; CSP(S), iii, pp. (Drury to Privy Council, 3rd and 9 April 1571).

6. Calderwood, iii, pp.55, 57.
7. Calderwood, iii, p.56.
8. CSP(S), iv, p.586 (Killigrew to Burghley and Leicester, 13 June 1573); Bannatyne, pp.107f. The spoils included:
(A) a great culverin, mounted for the walls and not for the field.
(B) Two batteries mounted for the walls and not for the field.
(C) Two myons, one for the walls, one for either.
(D) Two Bretenie falcons, mounted for walls.
(E) A quarter falcon, mounted for the walls.
(F) Three 'hackbuts of fownd'.
(G) Eight callivers.
(H) Sixty spears.
(I) Ammunition for all the above.
(J) Three large barrels of cannon powder.
(K) Three barrels of culverin powder.
(L) Eight barrels of hackbut powder.
9. Calderwood, iii, p.57.
10. Hume, p.310; Bannatyne, p.106.

Chapter 5
CAPTAIN OF THE CRAG

1. In *Satirical Poems*, p.177. This ballad, written in February 1571 and always attributed to Kirkcaldy, is first mentioned in Bannatyne, pp.86-90: Grange 'made a rowstie [roaring] rhyme which went from hand to hand, wherein he reproached bitterly the lords maintainers of the King's authority, and aggredged the injuries alleged done to the Queen.'
2. Melville, p.101.
3. CSP(S), iii, p.527 (Randolph to Morton, 11 April 1571); p.626 (Drury to Burghley, 8 July 1571); *Miscellaneous Papers*, pp.59f. (Lethington to Archbishop Beaton, 1 October 1571).
4. Calderwood, iii, p.73; Bannatyne, pp.110, 112.
5. CSP(S), iii, p.544 (Herle to Burghley, 16 April 1571).
6. Donaldson, p.114.
7. Bannatyne, pp.110, 112, 113; *Historie*, p.73; Calderwood, iii, pp.60, 70.
8. *Diurnal*, p.210; *Historie*, p.74; Calderwood, iii, p.71; Hume, p.316.
9. Maitland to Beaton, 28 August 1571, *Miscellaneous Papers*, p.66.
10. Bannatyne, pp.114, 117, 120; Calderwood, iii, pp.72, 74.
11. Bannatyne, p.111; Calderwood, iii, p.60.
12. Bannatyne, pp.124, 175, 229; Melvill, pp.26f.
13. CSP(F) 1569-71, p.484 (Drury to Burghley, 1 July 1571).
14. CSP(S), iii, pp.567f (Grange to Morton, and Morton to Grange, 7 May 1571).
15. CSP(S), iii, pp. 572 (Morton to Grange, 13 May 1571); *Diurnal*, p.209; Calderwood, iii, p.100.
16. Calderwood, iii, p.75; Lynch, *Edinburgh*, p.133.
17. Bannatyne, p.122.
18. *Historie*, p.76; Calderwood, iii, p.76; Bannatyne, p. 123, 14 May 1571.

19. CSP(F) 1569-71, p.447 (Drury to the Privy Council, 17 May 1571); Hume, p.317; Diurnal, pp.190f; Calderwood, iii, p.18.

20. Bannatyne, p.133.

21. *Diurnal*, p.216.

22. CSP(S), iii, p.583 (Drury to the Privy Council, 23 May 1571); Bannatyne, p.134.

23. Bannatyne, pp.137f; *Diurnal*, pp.219f.

24. CSP(F) 1569-71, p.449 (Elizabeth to Drury, 20 May 1571).

25. CSP(S), iii, pp.588ff. (Maitland to Elizabeth, 30 May 1571).

26. CSP(S), iii, p.591 (Grange to Elizabeth, 30 May 1571).

27. CSP(S), iii, p.580 (Elizabeth to Drury, 20 May 1571).

28. CSP(S), iii, p.587 (Lennox to Elizabeth, 28 May 1571).

29. Lynch, *History*, p.221.

Chapter 6
THE DOUGLAS WARS BEGIN

1. *Historie*, p.103.

2. Bannatyne, p.137; *Diurnal*, pp.218f; Hume, pp.317f; Calderwood, iii, pp.89f; Grant, *Memoirs*, pp.268-272.

3. CSP(S), iii, p.602 (Drury to Burghley, 9 June 1571).

4. CSP(S), iii, p.533 (Diary of the Bishop of Ross, 3 July 1571); p.604 (Challenge by Grange, 11 June 1571); p.605 (Answer to Grange's Challenge, 14 June 1571) and p.611 (Lennox's Answer to Drury, June 1571); Bannatyne, pp.141-158; Calderwood, iii, pp.90f., 106-111.

5. CSP(S), iii, p.532 (Diary of the Bishop of Ross, 18 July 1571); p.608 (Drury to Burghley, 17 June 1571).

6. CSP(S), iii, p.605 (Parliament at Edinburgh, 13 June 1571).

7. Bannatyne, p.125; M'Crie, p.256.

8. Bannatyne, pp.138-141; Calderwood, iii, pp.76f; Kerr, p.96.

9. CSP(S), iii, p.532 (Diary of the Bishop of Ross, 16 June 1571); CSP(S), iii, p.608 (Drury to Burghley, 17 June 1571). Bannatyne, p.172; *Diurnal*, p.224; Calderwood, iii, pp.99ff; Hume, p.318ff.

10. CSP(S), iii, p.631 (Drury to Burghley, 24 July 1571); Maxwell, p.138; *Diurnal*, p.226; Lynch, *Edinburgh*, p.132.

11. CSP(S), iii, pp.618f. (Demands by Lennox; Memoranda for Lennox, June 1571).

12. CSP(S), iii, p.532 (Diary of the Bishop of Ross, 12 July 1571); pp.620ff (Drury to Burghley, 4 and 6 July 1571); *Diurnal*, pp.229f; Holinshed, v, p.651.

13. CSP(S), iii, pp.672 & 676 (Drury to Burghley, 1 and 4 September 1571); Calderwood, iii, p.138.

14. CSP(S), iii, p.630 (Drury to Burghley, 15 July 1571); *Diurnal*, p.234 (20 and 25 July 1571).

15. Bannatyne, p.176.

16. CSP(S), iii, p.664 (Drury to Burghley, 24 August 1571); *Diurnal*, pp.239f.

17. *Historie*, p.87.

18. *Diurnal*, p.242; Calderwood, iii, p.136; CSP(S), iii, p.678 (Case to Drury, 2 September 1571).

19. *Historie*, p.88.

Chapter 7
THE STIRLING RAID

1. CSP(F) 1569-71 (Hunsdon to Lethington and Grange, 5 November 1571).
2. *Historie*, p.91.
3. The most authoritative account is Grange's own: CSP(F), 1569-71, p.526 (Grange and Lethington to Drury, 6 September 1571); Hume, p.321; Melville, p.91.
4. CSP(S), iii, p.676 (Advertisements from Scotland, 4 September 1571). Calderwood, iii, p.138 says the Castilians had about 200 horse and 300 foot.
5. *Diurnal*, p.248; Bannatyne, p.184.
6. CSP(S), iii, p.681 (to Burghley, 5 September 1571); p.700 (Second Deposition of George Bell, 6 September 1571).
7. Grant, *Memoirs*, p.284, citing Nimmo's *History of Stirlingshire*.
8. CSP(S), iii, p.681 (to Burghley, 5 September 1571), p.697 (Drury to Burghley, 13 September 1571); iv, 232 (Randolph and Drury to the Lords of Edinburgh Castle, 17 April 1572); CSP(F) 1569-71, p.533 (First and Second Examination of Bell, 5 and 6 September 1571, Examination of Calder, 6 September 1571); Calderwood, iii, p.140.
9. CSP(S), iii, p.687 (Grange and Maitland to Drury, 6 September 1571).
10. CSP(F), 1569-71, p.523 (to Drury, 4 September, 1571).
11. CSP(S), iii, pp.685ff (Grange and Maitland to Drury, 6 September 1571).

Chapter 8
MONEY IS THE MAN

1. CSP(S), iii, p.697 (Drury to Burghley, 14 September 1571).
2. CSP(S), iii, p.682 (Maitland to Mary, 5 September 1571).
3. CSP(S), iv, p.4 (Drury to Burghley, 9 October 1571); p.8 (John Case's Dealings, 13 October 1571); p.56 (Hunsdon to the Privy Council, 27 November 1571); *Diurnal*, p.251f.
4. Calderwood, iii, p.153.
5. CSP(S), iii, p.697 (Drury to Burghley, 13 September 1571); iv, pp7f. (John Case's Dealings, 13 October 1571); p.12 (Drury to the Privy Council, 15 October 1571); p.53 (Ordnance etc for the Assault on Edinburgh Castle, November 1571); *Diurnal*, pp.227, 231; Maxwell, p.138, Bannatyne, pp.192-195.
6. CSP(S), iv, p.15 (Drury to Burghley, 19 October 1571); *Diurnal*, pp.250f.
7. Bannatyne, p.213.
8. CSP(S), iv, pp.18-21 (Instructions for Lord Hunsdon, 22 October 1571).
9. CSP(S), iv, pp.45-56 (Instructions to Andrew Melville, 18 November 1571; Morton's Demands, 25 November, Hunsdon to Privy Council, Burghley, and Elizabeth, 16, 22, 27 and 28 November 1571).
10. RPC(S), ii, pp.85f. (Leith, 24 October 1571).
11. RPC(S), ii, p.104 (Morton, 25 December 1571).
12. CSP(F) 1569-71, p.558 (Hunsdon to Burghley, 11 November 1571).
13. CSP(S), iv, p.66 (Hunsdon to Burghley, 14 December 1571); *Diurnal*, p.285. Calderwood, iii, p.166.
14. Melville, p.93.

Chapter 9
DIVIDED IN MINDS

1. *Historie*, p.74.
2. CSP(F) 1572-74, p.55 (Hunsdon to Elizabeth, 8 March 1572).
3. CSP(S), iii, p.704 (Elizabeth to Mar, 30 January 1572); iv, p.111 (Anjou to Maitland, 7 February 1572).
4. CSP(S), iv, pp.93ff. (Elizabeth's Advice for Ending the War in Scotland, 22 January 1572); p.96 (Hunsdon to Burghley, 26 January 1572); pp.100ff. (Articles for Reducing Scotland to Peace, 31 January 1572).
5. Hume, p.324; *Diurnal*, p.287; *Biographical Sketches*, p.125; CSP(S), iv, p.136. (Advices from Scotland, 26 February 1572); CSP(F) 1572-74, p.105 (Hunsdon to Burghley, 9 May 1572).
6. CSP(S), iv, p.173 (Drury and Randolph to Hunsdon, 19 March 1572); *Diurnal*, pp.259f, 290.
7. CSP(S), iv, p.112 (Hunsdon to Burghley, 11 February 1572).
8. CSP(S), iv, pp.129ff. (Drury and Randolph to Hunsdon, 23 February 1572); p.146 (Randolph to Leicester, 6 March 1572).
9. CSP(S), iv, p.132 (Hunsdon to Drury and Randolph, 24 February 1572); Lynch, Edinburgh, p.205.
10. CSP(S), iv, p.339 (Drury to Burghley, 27 June 1572); *Diurnal*, pp.291, 297f; *Historie*, p.106; Smith, pp.25f; Lynch, *History*, p.222; Murray, pp.48,51.
11. RPC(S), ii, p.132 (Leith 4 April 1572); CSP(S), iv, p.377 (Maitland to Mary, 10 August 1572); *Diurnal*, pp.262, 296; Grant, *Memorials*, p.109.
12. CSP(S), iv, p.133 (Drury and Randolph to Hunsdon, 26 February 1572); CSP(F) 1572-74, p.48 (Advices from Scotland, 26 February 1572); *Diurnal*, pp.257, 289, 293, 295, 303; *Historie*, p.103; Calderwood, iii, pp.212ff; Lynch, *Edinburgh*, p.139 and *History*, p.221.
13. CSP(F) 1572-74, p.76 (Randolph and Drury to Hunsdon, 10 April 1572); pp.131, 133 (Drury to Hunsdon, and to Burghley 14 and 21 June 1572); *Diurnal*, pp.299, 302, 306.
14. CSP(S), iv, p.173 (Drury and Randolph to Hunsdon, 19 March 1572); p.209 (Thomas Smith and Walsingham to Elizabeth, 3 April 1572).
15. CSP(S), iv, pp.193ff; ('Demands of those in the Castle,' 'Pacification of Scotland,' Drury and Randolph to Hunsdon, and Drury to Burghley 28 and 31 March 1572).
16. CSP(S), iv, p.233 (Hunsdon to Burghley, 18 April 1572) gives the day as Monday 14 but Drury himself says it was Sunday 13 and he ought to know – p.246 (Drury to Hunsdon, 18 April 1572).
17. CSP(S), iv, p.352 (Drury to Hunsdon, 12 July 1572).
18. CSP(S), iv, p.320 (Drury to Hunsdon, 7 June 1572).
19. Bannatyne, p.232; Calderwood, iii, p.213; *Diurnal*, p.262.
20. CSP(S), iv, p.319 (Drury to Hunsdon, 7 June 1572).
21. CSP(S), iv, p.319 (Drury to Hunsdon, 7 June 1572).
22. *Historie*, pp.105f.
23. CSP(S), iv, pp.322-330 (Drury to Burghley, 10, 11, 12 and 14 June 1572); Calderwood, iii, p.213.
24. *Diurnal*, pp.263ff; Lynch, *Edinburgh*, p.141.
25. CSP(S), iv, pp.233f. (Hunsdon to Elizabeth and to Burghley, 18 April 1572), 236 (Drury and Randolph to Hunsdon, 17 April 1572); p.245 (Drury to Hunsdon, 18 April 1572).

26. CSP(F) 1572-74, p.55 (Hunsdon to Elizabeth, 8 March 1572); CSP(S), iv, p.233 (Hunsdon to Burghley, 18 April 1572).
27. CSP(S), iv, pp.334f (Proclamation of the Regent Mar, and Drury to Hunsdon, 21 June 1572); RPC(S), ii, p.148 (Leith, 21 June 1572); *Diurnal*, p.302.
28. CSP(S), iv, p.346 (Advertisements of Scottish Affairs, 3 July 1572).
29. CSP(S), iv, p.350 (Drury to Burghley, 8 July 1572).
30. CSP(S), iv, p.352 (Drury to Hunsdon, 12 July 1572); p.354 (Drury to Burghley, 16 July 1572); Bannatyne, p.237.
31. CSP(S), iv, p.335 (Maitland and Grange's Answer to Errington, 26 June 1572).
32. CSP(F) 1572-74, p.143 (Drury to Burghley, 8 July 1572).
33. CSP(S), iv, pp.363f. (Form of the Abstinence, 30 July 1572); Calderwood, iii, pp.215-218, Tytler, p.77.
34. CSP(F) 1572-74, p.152 (Conference between Tullibardine and Lethington and Grange, 18 July 1572).
35. CSP(F) 1572-74, p.150 (Lethington and Grange to Drury, 16 July 1572); CSP(S), iv, p.376 (Maitland to Mary, 10 August 1572).

Chapter 10
LED UPON THE ICE

1. *Historie*, p.119.
2. Bannatyne, p.247.
3. CSP(S), iv, p.440 (Penitents Received into the Kirk, November 1572); Lynch, *History*, p. 221.
4. Bannatyne, p.255.
5. CSP(S), iv, p.375 (Maitland and Grange to Drury, 8 August 1572); p.379 (Mar to Drury, 15 August 1572); p.383 (Drury to Burghley, 27 August 1572); p.708 (Drury to Mar, 13 August 1572); p.710 (Elizabeth to Mar, August 1572); CSP(F) 1572-74, p.170 (Drury to Burghley, 20 August 1572).
6. CSP(F) 1572-74, p.187 (Proclamation, 3 October 1572).
7. CSP(S), iv, p.398 (Killigrew to Burghley and Leicester, 19 September 1572); Bannatyne, p.273.
8. CSP(S), iv, pp.385f. (Instructions to Killigrew, August 1572); pp.399f. (Killigrew to Burghley and Leicester, 19 September 1572).
9. Melville, p.247.
10. Cited in Donaldson, p.122.
11. CSP(S), iv, p.427 (Notes given to Killigrew, 28 October 1572).
12. Tytler, p.87; M'Crie, p.273; Melville, p.27.

Chapter 11
MORTON'S MANOEUVRES

1. CSP(S), iv, p.467 (Alexander Hay to Killigrew, 17 January 1573).
2. CSP(S), iv, p.469 (Maitland and Grange to De La Mothe, 17 January 1573).
3. CSP(S), iv, p.439 (Reasons why the Regent cannot allow the Castle's Demands, November 1572); pp.453f. (Renewal of the War, 1 January 1573).
4. Melville, p.249f.

5. Melville, pp.251;Tytler, p.88.
6. Tytler, p.86.
7. CSP(S), iv, pp.463f., 469f. (Maitland and Grange to Mary and to De La Mothe, 14 and 17 January 1573).
8. CSP(S), iv, p.443 (Killigrew to Burghley 10 December 1572).
9. CSP(S), iv, pp.455-60 (Killigrew to Thomas Smith, 7 January 1573); p.515 (Discourse by the Regent Morton, 13 March 1573).

Chapter 12
SAFE FROM NO MAN'S CURSING

1. CSP(F) 1572-74, p.273 (Killigrew to Burghley, 4 March 1573).
2. CSP(F) 1572-74, p.300 (Killigrew to Burghley, 4 April 1573).
3. CSP(S), iv, p.455 (Morton to Killigrew, 6 January 1573); p.459 (Killigrew to Sir Thomas Smith, 7 January 1573).
4. CSP(S), iv, p.468 (Alexander Hay to Killigrew, 17 January 1573); *Diurnal*, p.323; Hume, p.326; Holinshed, v, p.668; *J&S*, p.74; Lynch, *Edinburgh*, p.144.
5. CSP(F) 1572-74, p.236 (Killigrew to Burghley, 25 January 1573).
6. CSP(S), iv, p.474 (Killigrew to Burghley, 25 January 1573); pp.475f. (Survey of Edinburgh, 26 January 1573); p.478 (Killigrew to Burghley, 29 January 1573); *Accounts*, xii, p.346; *J&S*, p.69.
7. CSP(S), iv, p.483 (Killigrew to Burghley, 1 February 1573); p.486 (Killigrew to Thomas Smyth, 5 February 1573), p.490 (Advices out of Scotland, February 1573); pp.494f. (Wants for Service in Scotland, February 1573).
8. CSP(S), iv, p.474 (Killigrew to Burghley, 25 January 1573; p.482 (News out of Scotland, 29 January 1573); p.490 (Advices out of Scotland, February 1573); Hume, p.326; Holinshed, v, p.669; Oldtrieve, p.243.
9. CSP(S), iv, p.477 (James Kirkcaldy to Huntly, 27 January 1573); p.478 (Killigrew to Burghley, 29 January 1573); p.499 (Lethington and Grange to Huntly, 23 February 1573); Tytler, p.89.
10. CSP(S), iv, p.484 (Maitland to Huntly, 1 February 1573); pp.486f (Killigrew to Thomas Smyth, 5 February 1573), pp.487, 490 (Advices out of Scotland, February 1573); Hume, p.325; Calderwood, iii, p.260; Spottiswoode gives a very different account, ii, pp.189f.
11. CSP(S), iv, p.490 (Advices out of Scotland, February 1573); *Historie*, p.128; Hume, p.326; Calderwood, iii, p.261; Grant, *Memorials*, p.110.
12. CSP(S), iv, p.492 (William Wardall to Huntingdon, 19 February 1573).
13. CSP(S), iv, pp.495-98 (Submission of Huntly and the Hamiltons, 23 February 1573). p.515 (Discourse by Morton, 13 March 1573); p.523 (Huntly to Henry Killigrew, 23 March 1573); Melville, pp.252f.
14. CSP(S), iv, p.492 (Killigrew to Smyth, 18 February 1573).
15. CSP(S), iv, p.523 (Maitland to Lady Livingston, N.D., 1573).
16. CSP(S), iv, p.503 (Killigrew to Smyth, 26 February 1573); p.520 (Killigrew to Burghley, March 17 1573); Tytler, p.89.
17. CSP(S), iv, pp.511f (Drury and Killigrew to Burghley, 7 and 9 March 1573); p.514 (Commission by Elizabeth to Drury, 12 March 1573).
18. CSP(S), iv, p.511; CSP(F) 1572-74; p.293 (Errington to Drury, 5 and 27 March 1573).
19. CSP(S), iv, p.52ff and 533 (Killigrew to Burghley, and to Maitland and Grange, 27 March 1573; Errington's Report, March 1573).

20. CSP(S), iv, pp.534ff. (Errington's Report and Occurrences in Scotland, 30 March 1573).

21. Oldtrieve, p.267.

22. CSP(S), iv, p.529 (Morton's Answer to Drury, 28 March 1573); pp.547ff. (Contract between Drury and Ruthven, 17 April 1573, and Hostages for Elizabeth's Security, 18 April 1573); RPC(S), ii, pp.216f. (Edinburgh, 17 April 1573); p.55 (Morton to the Town of Edinburgh, 2 May 1573).

23. CSP(S), iv, pp.531, 536 (Killigrew to Burghley, 29 March 1573, Occurrences in Scotland, 30 March 1573).

24. CSP(S), iv, p.543 (Drury to Burghley, 11 April 1573); Warrender, p.120.

25. CSP(S), iv, pp.531, 536 (Killigrew to Burghley, 29 March 1573); pp.537f. (Killigrew, and Drury to Burghley, 4 April 1573); p.540 (Killigrew to Burghley and Leicester, 7 April 1573); CSP(F) 1572-74, pp. 314, 342 (Killigrew to Burghley, 17 April and 22 May 1573).

26. CSP(S), iv, p.553 (Killigrew to Burghley, 27 April 1573); p.556 (Names of those in Edinburgh Castle, 1 May 1573); J&S, pp.72, 80.

27. Grant, *Memoirs*, p.376. According to an inventory made shortly after the siege, over forty artillery pieces were found. Given that several were destroyed during the siege, the Castilians probably had in the region of fifty pieces of ordnance, or one for every three men in the garrison!

28. CSP(S), iv, pp.552f (Summons by James VI to Grange, 25 April 1573); pp.552f. (News from Scotland, and Killigrew to Burghley, 27 April 1573).

29. CSP(S), iv, pp.539, 552 (Killigrew to Burghley, 17 and 27 April 1573).

30. CSP(S), iv, p.556 (Killigrew to Leicester, 2 May 1573).

31. Tytler, p.90.

32. CSP(S), iv, pp.559f. (Band Between the Town and the Castle of Edinburgh, 8 May 1573); Bannatyne, pp.163f.

Chapter 13
LIKE SNAIL IN SHELL

1. Thomas Churchyard, 'The Siege of Edinburgh Castle' in *Satirical Poems*, pp.274, 281.

2. CSP(F) 1572-74, p.331(Killigrew to Burghley, 5 May 1573); CSP(S), iv, p.562 (Killigrew to Burghley, 12 May 1573); J&S, pp.72ff.

3. CSP(S), iv, p.572 (Names of those in Edinburgh Castle when it surrendered, 28 May 1573); Hume, p.327; Grant, *Memorials*, p.111; Birrel, p.20f.

4. CSP(S), iv, p.564 (Killigrew to Burghley, 17 May 1573).

5. CSP(S), iv, p.565 (Drury to Burghley, 18 May 1573).

6. CSP(S), iv, p.564 (Killigrew to Burghley, 17 May 1573).

7. CSP(S), iv, pp.567f. (Killigrew & Cotton to Burghley, 22 and 23 May 1573); p.579 (Drury to Burghley, 5 June 1573); J&S, p.75; Hume, p.327.

8. CSP(F) 1572-74 p.343 (Drury to Burghley, 23 May 1573); *Diurnal*, p.332; Hume, p.327; Grant, *Memorials*, p.113; J&S, p.69; Oldtrieve, pp.230, 243, 256, see plan on p.268.

9. CSP(S), iv, p.570 (Drury to Burghley, 28 May 1573); Hume, pp.327f.

10. CSP(S), iv, p.570 (Killigrew to Burghley and Leicester, 27 May 1573, and Drury to Burghley, 28 May 1573).

11. CSP(S), iv, p.571 (Conditions of the Surrender of Edinburgh Castle, 28 May 1573).

12. CSP(S), iv, p.572 (Names of those in Edinburgh Castle when it surrendered, 28 May 1573); p.579 (Drury to Burghley, 5 June 1573); p.590 (Remembrance for Burghley, 20 June 1573).
13. Grant, *Memorials*, pp.116ff.
14. CSP(S), iv, p.590 (Remembrance for Burghley, 20 June 1573); Grant, *Memorials*, p.114.
15. CSP(S), iv, p.604 (Morton to Countess of Lennox, 5 August 1573).

Chapter 14
A JUST RECOMPENSE

1. CSP(S), iv, p.516 (Discourse by Morton, 13 March 1573).
2. CSP(F) 1572-74, p.353 (Drury to Burghley, 1 June 1573); CSP(S), iv, p.579 (Killigrew to Thomas Smith, 5 June 1573); Hume, p.329.
3. CSP(S), iv, pp.573, 577f. (Maitland and Grange to Burghley and to Leicester, 29 May and 1 June 1573); p.581 (Thomas Cecil to Burghley, 7 June 1573).
4. CSP(S), iv, p.574 (Morton to Burghley, 31 May 1573); Tytler, p.91.
5. CSP(S), iv, pp.581ff., 599 (Elizabeth to Drury, and to Killigrew, and to Morton, 8, 9 and 19 June 1573).
6. *Diurnal*, p.334; CSP(S), iv, pp.582, 583, 595 (Elizabeth to Morton, 9 June 1573, Killigrew to Burghley, 12 June 1573, Morton to the Countess of Lennox, June 1573); Hume, p.329; Melville, p.101.
7. CSP(S), iv, pp.588, 591, 600 (Drury to Burghley, 18 June 1573, Mary Fleming to Burghley, 21 June 1573, Elizabeth to Morton, 19 July 1573); CSP(F), 1572-1574, no.1044; Calderwood, iii, p.285.
8. CSP(F) 1572-74, p.401 (Offers for Grange's Life, August 1573); CSP(S), iv. pp.601f. (Captain Cockburn and Morton to Killigrew, 1 and 5 August 1573); Tytler p.93.
9. CSP(S), (Killigrew to Burghley, 3 August 1573); Calderwood, iii, pp.284f.
10. Calderwood, iii, p.285; Lynch, *History*, p.226.
11. Hume, p.329.
12. *Accounts*, xii, p.270.
13. RPS, vii, p.1528 (24 March 1578).
14. Melville, p.102.

BIBLIOGRAPHY

History is written by the winners and many of the accounts of particular military engagements must inevitably exaggerate the prowess of the one side and the wretchedness of the other. According to most contemporary accounts – and those by Bannatyne and some of the English observers are particularly partisan – as well as later narratives by the likes of Calderwood and Hume of Godscroft – the Castilians hardly ever won a skirmish and frequently lost large numbers of men. This squares ill with the determined resistance they put up to the forces of successive regents over a period of three years. The anonymous authors of the *Diurnal of Occurrents* and the *Historie of James Sext* present a more balanced picture in their chronicles.

I Printed Primary and Early Historical Works

Accounts of the Lord High Treasurer of Scotland, 12 vols, Edinburgh 1907-1970, vol. XII (1566-1574), edited by Charles McInnes, Edinburgh, 1970.

Bannatyne, Richard, *Memorials of Transactions in Scotland*, 1569-1573, edited by R. Pitcairn, 1836.
The Bannatyne Miscellany, edited by David Laing, 3 vols, 1836, vol. ii, pp.65-80:
   'A Survey of the castle and town of Edinburgh, January 1573.'
   'Journal of the siege of Edinburgh Castle, April-May 1573.'
Birrel, Robert, *Diary 1532-1605*, in *Fragments of Scottish History*, edited by John Dalzell, 1798.
The Border Papers, vol. I (1550-1594), edited by Joseph Bain, Edinburgh, 1894.
Bourne, William, *The Arte of Shooting in Great Ordnaunce*, London, 1587.
Buchanan, George, *The History of Scotland* translated from the Latin by James Aikman, 2 vols, London, 1827-1829.

Calderwood, David, *History of the Kirk*, 8 vols, edited by T. Thompson, Edinburgh, 1842-49.
Calendar of State Papers (Foreign Series),
   1569-1571, edited by Allan Crosby, London, 1874.
   1572-74, edited by Allan Crosby, 1876.
Calendar of State Papers relating to Scottish Affairs,
   Vol. II (1563-69), edited by Joseph Bain, Edinburgh, 1900.
   Vol. III (1569-71) edited by William Boyd, Edinburgh, 1903.

Vol. IV (1571-74) edited by William Boyd, Edinburgh, 1905.

Dalyell, John Graham, *Scottish Poems of the Sixteenth Century*, 2 vols, Edinburgh, 1801.

A Diurnal of Remarkable Occurrents in Scotland since the Death of King James IV till the Year MDLXXV, from a ms of the Sixteenth Century, edited by T. Thompson, Edinburgh, 1833.

Extracts from the Records of the Burgh of Edinburgh, edited by J.D. Marwick and M.Wood, 6 vols, Edinburgh, Scottish Burgh Record Society, 1869-92, 1927.

Historie and Life of King James the Sext, Bannatyne Club, Edinburgh, 1825.

Holinshed, Raphael, *The Chronicles of England, Scotland and Ireland*, 6 vols, 1577, edited by H. Ellis, London, 1807-08.

Hume, David of Godscroft, *History of the House and Race of Douglas and Angus*, 2 vols, London, 1644.

Knox, J. *Works*, edited by D. Laing, 1846-64.
   History of the Reformation in Scotland, 2 vols, translated and edited by W. Croft Dickinson, Edinburgh, 1949.

Maxwell, John, Lord Herries, *Historical Memoirs of the Reign of Mary Queen of Scots*, edited by R̃. Pitcairn, Edinburgh, 1836.

Melvill, James, *Autobiography and Diary*, edited by R. Pitcairn, Edinburgh, Woodrow Society, 1842.

Melville, Sir James of Halhill, *Memoirs*, Bannatyne Club Edinburgh, 1827.

Miscellaneous Papers Principally Illustrative of events in the reigns of Queen Mary and James VI, edited by Andrew MacGeorge, Glasgow, 1834.

Moryson, Fynes, *An Itinerary of Fynes Moryson containing his ten years travel through the twelve dominions of Germany*, London, 1617.

Register of the Privy Council of Scotland.
   Vol. II (1569-78), edited by J.H. Burton, Edinburgh, 1878.
Register of the Privy Seal of Scotland.
   Vol. VI (1567-74) edited by G. Donaldson, Edinburgh, 1963.
   Vol. VII (1575-80) edited by G. Donaldson, Edinburgh, 1966.

Spottiswoode, John, *History of the Church of Scotland*, reprinted in 3 vols, 1668, Bannatyne Club, Edinburgh, 1850.

The Warrender Papers, 2 vols, edited by Anne Cameron, Scottish History Society, 1932.

II SECONDARY WORKS

Biographical Sketches of Sir William Kirkcaldy of Grange, in Dalyzell's *Scottish Poems*, pp.112-135.

Blackmore, H.L., *The Armouries of the Tower of London*, HMSO.

Blake, William, *William Maitland of Lethington, 1528-1573, A Study of the Policy of Moderation in the Scottish Reformation*, Queenstown, Ontario, 1990.

Caldwell, David (editor), *Scottish Weapons and Fortifications* 1100-1800, Edinburgh, 1981.

Cant, Ronald, and Ian Lindsay, *Old Stirling*, Edinburgh, 1948.

Cavers, Keith, *A Vision of Scotland: The Nation observed by John Slezer*, HMSO, 1993.

Cowan, Ian, 'The Marian Civil War 1567-1573,' in *Scotland and War AD79-1918*, edited by Norman MacDougall, Edinburgh, 1991, pp.95-112.

Cranstoun, James, *Satirical Poems from the Time of the Reformation*, Scottish Text Society Old Series, Edinburgh, 1891-93.

Dennison, Pat, and Russell Coleman, *Historic Dumbarton*, Historic Scotland, East Linton, 1999.

Donaldson, Gordon, *All the Queen's Men*, London, 1983.

Driscoll, Stephen and Peter Yeoman, *Excavations within Edinburgh Castle in 1988-91*, Society of the Antiquaries of Scotland, monograph series, Edinburgh, 1997.

Fawcett, Richard, *Edinburgh Castle*, 1980.

Ffoulkes, Charles, *The Gun-Founders of England*, Cambridge, 1937.

Goodare, Julian, *State and Society in Early Modern Scotland*, Oxford, 1999.

Graham, Roderick, *John Knox Democrat*, London, 2001.

Grant, James, *Memoirs and Adventures of Sir William Kirkaldy of Grange*, Edinburgh, 1849.
Memorials of the Castle of Edinburgh, Edinburgh, 1850.

Hewit, George, *Scotland under Morton 1572-80*, Edinburgh, 1982.

Kerr, T. Angus, 'The Later Ministry of John Craig at St Giles, 1567-1572,' in *SCHS*, pp.81-99.

Lee, Maurice, *James Stewart, Earl of Moray*, New York, 1953.
John Maitland of Thirlestane and the Foundation of the Stewart Despotism in Scotland, Princeton, 1959.

Lynch, *Edinburgh and the Reformation*, Edinburgh, 1981.
History of Scotland, Pimlico edn, London, 1992.

M'Crie, Thomas, *Life of John Knox*, Edinburgh, 1811.

MacDougall, Norman, *Scotland at War*, Edinburgh, 1991.

MacIvor, Iain, *Edinburgh Castle*, Batsford, 1981.

MacPhail, I.M.M., *Dumbarton Castle*, Edinburgh, 1979.

Mathieson, William, *Law, Politics and Religion, A Study in Scottish History from the Reformation to the Revolution*, 2 vols, Glasgow, 1902.

Murray, Joan, 'The Coinage of the Marians in Edinburgh Castle in 1572,' *British Numismatic Journal*, 57, 1987, pp.47-53.

Norman, A.V.B., and Don Pottinger, *English Weapons and Warfare 449-1660*, London, 1979.

Oldrieve, W.T., 'Account of the Discovery of the Remains of David's Tower,' *Proceedings of the Society of Antiquaries*, 1914, pp.230-270

Potter, Harry, *Blood Feud: The Stewarts and Gordons at War*, Tempus, 2002.

Russell, Ernest, *Maitland of Lethington*, London, 1912

Smith, Donald, *John Knox House*, Edinburgh, 1996.

Tabraham, Chris, *Scotland's Castles*, Historic Scotland, 1997.
Tytler, Patrick, *History of Scotland*, Edinburgh, 1841, new and enlarged edition in four volumes, London, 1877.

LIST OF ILLUSTRATIONS

21   Lord Claud Hamilton, attributed to Arnold Bronkhorst, by courtesy of the Duke of Abercorn.
22   The High Kirk of St Giles, author's photograph.
23   Mons Meg, author's photograph.
24   The Netherbow Port, c.1764, by courtesy of Edinburgh City Libraries.
25   A demi-culverin, c.1570 at Pevensey Castle, by courtesy of English Heritage Photo Library.
26   The Siege of Leith, 1560, by courtesy of Lord Egremont.
27   Sir Thomas Kerr of Fernihurst. Of unknown provenance.
28   Reconstruction of Holyrood Palace, c.1560, by David Simon.
29   James VI aged six, by Arnold Bronckhorst, courtesy of the Scottish National Portrait Gallery.
30   Map of Old Stirling.
31   Prospect of Stirling from the east by John Slezer, by courtesy of the Trustees of the National Library of Scotland.
32   Mar's Wark, from an eighteenth-century print of unknown provenance.
33   John Erskine, 1st Earl of Mar (Regent of Scotland) by John Scougall after an unknown artist, courtesy of the Scottish National Portrait Gallery.
34   Edinburgh, prospect from North, by John Slezer, courtesy of the Trustees of the National Library of Scotland.
35   The Flodden Wall on the west side of the Pleasance. Author's photograph.
36   Lord Hunsdon, by Marcus Gheeraerts, by courtesy of the Berkeley Castle Charity and by permission of the Courtauld Institute.
37   Edinburgh, prospect from the Dean, by John Slezer, by courtesy of the Trustees of the National Library of Scotland.
38   The South Side of the Castle by John Slezer, by courtesy of the Trustees of the National Library of Scotland.
39   Lord Seton by Frans Pourbus the Elder, by courtesy of the Scottish National Portrait Gallery.
40   Coins struck at Dalkeith, by courtesy of the National Museums of Scotland.
41   Blackness Castle, author's photograph.
42   Knox being helped from St Giles to the Netherbow, by courtesy of John Knox House.
43   Reconstruction of Edinburgh Castle in 1573, by David Simon.
44   A sixteenth-century cannon.
45   Assorted infantry and cavalrymen of the period.
46   The Regent Morton, courtesy of the Scottish National Portrait Gallery.
47   Prospect of the Castle and City from the Nor Loch, John Slezer, by courtesy of the Trustees of the National Library of Scotland.
48   Detail of the Siege, by courtesy of Edinburgh City Libraries.
49   The view of fire down Castlehill, author's photograph.
50   Gun loop in David's Tower, author's photograph.
51   The Siege of Edinburgh Castle, 1573, by courtesy of Edinburgh City Libraries.
52   A cannon and its appurtenances.
53   Detail showing the King's Mount, by courtesy of Edinburgh City Libraries.
54   The South Side of the Castle of Edinburgh, showing the vantage point from Drury's Mount, by courtesy of Edinburgh City Libraries.
55   Detail of the Siege, showing the Spur, by courtesy of Edinburgh City Libraries.

BIOGRAPHICAL INDEX

A

Alva, Ferbanando Alvarez de Toledo
(*c.*1507-1582), Duke of, Spanish General
in the Netherlands, 45, 46, 100, 144.

Angus, Earl of (see Douglas).

Arbroath, Commendator of
(see Hamilton, John)

Argyll, Earls of (see Campbell).

Arran, Earls of (see Hamilton).

Athol, Earls of (see Stewart).

B

Balfour, Sir James, of Pittendreich,
(*c.*1525-1583), politician and jurist, Clerk
Register of Scotland (1566), Keeper of
Edinburgh Castle, 16, 31,
95, 125

Bannatyne, Richard, (d.1605), secretary to
John Knox, 10, 38, 61, 63, 88.

Bargany, Laird of, (see Kennedy).

Beaton, David (1494-1546), Cardinal, 10.

Bell, George (ex. 1571), 78f, 82.

Bothwell, Earl of (see Hepburn).

Boyd, Robert (*c.*1517-1590), 4th Baron
Boyd (*c.*1557), 36, 77 139.

Brand, John, minister of the Canongate,
107.

Brickwell, Captain, 122, 134.

Bruce, James, Captain, 59, 102.

Buchan, Earl of (see Douglas, Robert).

Buchanan, George (1506-1582), scholar,
historian, Reformer, 38, 54 (illus 29),
55, 59.

Buccleugh (see Scott).

Burghley (see Cecil).

C

Caithness, Earls of (see Sinclair).

Calder, Captain James (ex. 1571), 82.

Calderwood, David (1575-1650), historian,
38, 55, 57, 145.

Campbell, Archibald (1530-1573), 5th Earl
of Argyll (1558), 11, 24-31, 33, 35, 46,
56, 67, 77.

Carey, George (1547-1603), 2nd Baron
Hunsdon (1598), 130, 135.

Carey, Henry (*c.*1524-1596), 1st Baron
Hunsdon (1559), Warden of the East
Marches, Governor of Berwick (1568),
first cousin of Elizabeth, 40, 78, 88, 89
(illus 36), 90, 93, 100, 103.

Cassilis, Earls of (see Kennedy).

Cathcart, Alan (1537-1618), 4th Baron
(1547), 79.

Cecil, Thomas (1542-1623), 2nd Baron
Burghley (1598), Earl of Exeter (1605),
130.

Cecil, William, (1520-1598), Lord Burghley
(1571), 33, 41, 44, 97, 110, 121, 143.

Charles IX, King of France (1560-1574),
45, 52, 56, 100, 105f, 109f, 151.

INDEX OF PLACES

GENERAL INDEX

A

Abstinence, or truce, (1571) 67, (1572), 93, 95;
    two-day truce (1572), 104;
    31 July 1572, 105-117.
Archaeological excavations, 115, 128f, 137.
Artillery (see Ordnance).

B

Black Parliament, 77.
Black Saturday, 73.
Blois, Treaty of (27 March 1572), 100.
Brechin, Battle of, 105.

C

Cannon, (see Ordnance)
Captain of the Chimneys, 98.
Carberry, battle of (15 June 1567), 11, 14.
Casket letters, 27.
Catholics, Papists, 9, 10, 13, 24, 36, 109f, 151.
Coining, 53, 59, 63.
Congregation, Lords of the, or Confederate Lords, 10f, 14.
Crabstone, battle of (1571), 88.
Craigmillar Conference (1566), 13.
Creeping Parliament (1571), 64.

D

Diurnal of Occurents, 34, 98, 104.
Douglas Wars, 69-77, 102.

E

Edinburgh Band, 74.
England and the English, 12, 18, 27, 35, 40f, 61, 67, 88, 90, 100, 109, 116, 125, 127.
Exiles (see Leith).

F

Flodden, battle of (9 September 1513), 21, 131.
France and the French, 10, 36, 40, 42, 45, 51, 88, 106, 109f, 116f, 123f, 128, 141.

G

Golfing, 92.

H

Historie of James Sext, 98, 125.
Huguenots, 109, 151.

I

Inflation, 100.

K

King's or Regent's party (Jacobeans), 11f, 35f, 40ff, 45f, 51, 60, 63f, 84, 88, 92, 94, 97, 109,151f.
Kirk, 35, 48f.